PRAISE FOR
CHOOSE YOUR LIFE PURPOSES

"It is not hyperbole to say that *Choose Your Life Purposes* is a masterpiece. Certainly, it is Eric Maisel's *magnum opus*. I wish this had been around when I was a teenager and a confused, depressed young adult. In his usual empathic, encouraging, insightful way, Maisel puts forth an existential plan for living in a turbulent world. It's amazing how he can approach such 'heavy' subjects in such a readable way. Thank you, Eric!"

—Denise Beck-Clark, LCSW, MFA

"In an uncertain and changing world, *Choose Your Life Purposes* stands out as a guiding light, illuminating the path toward authentic self-discovery and purposeful living. Through its insightful exploration of the human experience, Dr. Maisel navigates the complexities of existence with clarity and wisdom and celebrates the inherent beauty of the human experience. Whether you're embarking on choosing your purposes for the first time or navigating the complexities of changing circumstances, this book offers invaluable insights and guidance to help you surf the waves of life with grace and intentionality. Prepare to be inspired, challenged, and ultimately transformed by the profound wisdom contained here. This book is not just a read; it's a journey—a journey toward a more purposeful, fulfilling, and authentic life."

—Elodie Desrumaux, artistic development coach

"*Choose Your Life Purposes* is a thought-provoking and empowering book. With wit and wisdom, Eric Maisel passionately challenges us to confront life's absurdity and embrace our autonomy and personal power in our role as steward of our own existence. He inspires us to live each day intentionally and to consciously choose our own purposes. It's a call

to discover or reconnect with our inner existentialist and a reminder that we get to be the pilot of our own journey!"

—**Jo Watson**, psychotherapist and founder of www. adisorder4everyone.com

"In a time in which people seem to have lost a sense of meaning and purpose, here is a book that is set to embolden and encourage the reader to take the reins back on life in practical, intuitive, and meaningful ways. In typical Maiselian fashion, there is no mucking about—no sugarcoating the trials and tribulations of life. However, his realistic and pragmatic views will resonate with you. *Choose Your Life Purposes* is sure to provide a much-needed existential jolt as you work to not only examine your life but also revise and hopefully succeed in revamping your own life philosophy."

—**Arnoldo Cantú**, editor of *Practical Alternatives to the Psychiatric Model*

"This book offers what it says on the cover with no holds barred. But Eric Maisel does it in the nicest way. There is no recourse to fancy theorizing, no display of erudition, just plain, unequivocal, common sense designed to move a person along in their life. Reading this book will stimulate the right kind of self-questioning. Reading it in a group with others who are in a similar 'stuck' position will help to get the creative juices going. This is a great contribution to the self-help literature!"

—**Richard Hallam**, author of *Abolishing the Concept of Mental Illness*

"Don't let Eric Maisel's engaging and accessible writing style fool you into thinking this is merely an easy read—there is both deep wisdom and practical advice in these pages. This book challenges you to take ownership of your life in a fresh way. Get it and read it now!"

—**Evan Mazunik**, composer, pianist, and creativity coach

"I believe that this book is a call to do what will save us emotionally, psychologically, and spiritually in the midst of these overwhelmingly complex times we are living in. Maisel not only tells us *why* we should live our life purposes but also shows us *how* to do this. Read this book for inspiration and hope—it will make a difference in your life!"

—**Lynda Monk**, director of the International Association for Journal Writing (IAJW.org)

"Eric Maisel has written another phenomenal book! His compassionate words zapped straight into my complicated, angst-ridden soul and soothed it within the first few paragraphs. I don't know how anything new can come from one author with so many books behind him, but he's done it again! If you seek to understand deeper meaning, you *need* this new guide."

—**Brenda Schweder**, found object artist

"In his new book, *Choose Your Life Purposes*, Eric Maisel describes a multidimensional path toward developing and maintaining a meaningful life. Fortunately for the reader, Maisel continues to live his life purposes as a writer, a philosopher, and a humanist. I recommend this book for people of any age—the young and the young at heart alike."

—**Susan Raeburn**, PhD, Creative Recovery

"Maisel rejects the existence of a higher truth than our own, instead supporting individuality, creativity, and personal courage and challenging the reader to assert meaning and to choose to 'act as if we matter.' Lucidly illustrating the many paradoxes inherent in living an examined life, Maisel exhorts his readers to identify and commit to living their life purposes, come what may. A heartfelt, provocative book!"

—**Anne M. Carley**, author, coach, and editor

"*Choose Your Life Purposes* by Eric Maisel is a delight. It delineates concepts central to life design: from the forms of personality and our human propensity for entanglement, to the value of excellence, deliberate ways of being, and experimentation. Readers can use *Choose Your Life Purposes* to become more self-aware, more deliberate, and more alive. Maisel's latest book manages to be both profound and practical. Maisel effortlessly explains how an existentialist life philosophy works with contemporary psychology to help people engage with their freedom in order to change. When folks ask me what existentialism is, or better yet, what it's for, I'll hand them this book. Reading Eric Maisel is enriching, illuminating, and joyous."

—**Kate Hammer**, existential therapist and coaching psychologist

"Eric Maisel's books have been instrumental in deepening my skills over my years seeing clients as an executive coach and creativity strategist. His new book *Choose Your Life Purposes* is one of the most useful books I've ever encountered on the subject of 'purpose.' Maisel covers not only practical methods and approaches to the topic, but more importantly, he lays down the foundations of a cognitive and affective framework that can serve as a strategic (and tactical) field manual to find/choose one's path in life. And he does this all in clear prose free of jargon and platitudes that characterize most books in the self-help and self-development genre today. Eric's experience, knowledge, and wisdom where it concerns the 'human condition' shine through. It's a book worth reading over and over."

—**Lon Fuentes**, executive coach and strategy consultant

"*Choose Your Life Purposes* is a life-changer. Better than that, it offers a new way of living, a new way of approaching life that is both sensible and exciting. Maisel provides a straightforward, accessible, and enlightening look at personality that provides us with a fresh approach to understanding human existence and what it means to be human. I think this cleverly written and understated exploration of meaning and purpose is in fact a movement that sheds light on a great new path forward, away from the darkness of chaos and crisis and into the light of active and meaningful living."

—**Sarah Clayton**, creativity coach, author *The Write Wild Method*

"Eric Maisel has developed an insightful and accessible guide for personal inspection and transformation. Maisel uses real-world examples to bring transformative change not only into the realm of the possible, but into the sphere of the practical as well. Unlike many seemingly similar books, *Choose Your Life Purposes* is easily adapted to the reader's current state and is rich with effective and engaging practices. The 'learning curve' has been replaced with a reusable 'learning experience.' I highly recommend you use Maisel's work to assess, plan, and carry out personal transformative change."

—**Greg Tutunjian**, agile performance coach

"As a creative, I have struggled most of my life with everything from what landscape to paint and what novel to read to what music to listen to and what to have for dinner, and everything in between. When choosing my life's purpose, well...that was an endeavor too enormous to think about. Or so I thought!

"Eric Maisel's *Choose Your Life Purposes* doesn't just provide steps; it offers clear, concrete, and, most importantly, practical steps that affirm I don't have to choose just *one* purpose but can (and perhaps should) entertain the multiple purposes I long to pursue. Maisel's very accessible writing style and numerous examples and scenarios make *Choose Your Life Purposes* a useful guidebook for anyone hesitating to take their next step or reaffirming their life's paths and journeys in their wake. Positive, powerful, and, yes, purposeful, Maisel's newest book fills a gap in the self-help and creativity literature."

—**B. Morey Stockwell**, PhD, author of *Do Your ART! 10 Simple Steps to Enhance Your Creativity and Elevate Your Mood*

"Eric Maisel's latest in a long series of helpful books offers practical and illuminating guidance for all of us who wonder how to discern the purpose and meaning of our lives. Combining a step-by-step process with deep discussions of life's persistent questions, Maisel's wisdom and occasional humor speak to us authentically. You need to read this book, preferably more than once, if you ever ask the question, 'What was I made for?' "

—**Lucy Freedman**, author of *Smart Work: The Syntax Guide to Influence* and developer of the course, "Showing Up to Be Who You Choose to Be"

"How do you intend to live? Isn't that a big, hairy question? And that is the question that Eric Maisel invites and guides you to answer in his book *Choose Your Life Purposes*. With this inspirational philosophy, Maisel introduces values-driven strategies so you can craft the project of your life by shifting from the idea that life has a purpose to the idea that you choose your life purposes. As a career and creativity coach, I have met a diverse range of clients who tell me they are seeking something more meaningful and purposeful—but they don't know what that something is or how to find it. I am recommending this book to all of my clients, especially those who want to intentionally live every day as the authors of their own success."

—**Sharon Stratford**, career and creativity coach

CHOOSE YOUR LIFE PURPOSES

Other Works by Eric Maisel

Nonfiction

Affirmations for Artists

Affirmations for Self-Love (with Lynda Monk)

The Art of the Book Proposal

Artists Speak

The Atheist's Way

Become a Creativity Coach Now!

Brainstorm

Coaching the Artist Within

Choose Your Life Purposes

Creative Recovery

The Creativity Book

Creativity for Life

Deep Writing

Everyday You

Fearless Creating

The Future of Mental Health

Helping Parents of Diagnosed, Distressed, and Different Children

Helping Survivors of Authoritarian Parents, Siblings, and Partners

Humane Helping

Life Purpose Boot Camp

The Life Purpose Diet

Lighting the Way

Living the Writer's Life

Making Your Creative Mark

Mastering Creative Anxiety

Overcoming Your Difficult Family

Parents Who Bully

Performance Anxiety

The Power of Daily Practice

Redesign Your Mind

Rethinking Depression

Secrets of a Creativity Coach

60 Innovative Cognitive Strategies for the Bright, the Sensitive, and the Creative

Sleep Thinking

Ten Zen Seconds

Toxic Criticism

20 Communication Tips at Work

20 Communication Tips
for Families

The Van Gogh Blues

Unleashing the Artist Within

What Would Your Character Do?

Why Smart, Creative and Highly
Sensitive People Hurt

Why Smart People Hurt

Why Smart Teens Hurt

Write Mind

Writers and Artists on Devotion

Writers and Artists on Love

A Writer's Paris

A Writer's San Francisco

A Writer's Space

Nonfiction (as editor)

Critiquing the Psychiatric Model
(editor, with Chuck Ruby)

Deconstructing ADHD

Hearing Critical Voices

Humane Alternatives to the
Psychiatric Model (editor, with
Chuck Ruby)

Inside Creativity Coaching

Practical Alternatives to the
Psychiatric Model of Mental
Illness (editor, with Arnoldo
Cantú and Chuck Ruby)

The Coaches Guide to Completing
Creative Work (editor, with
Lynda Monk)

The Creativity Workbook for
Coaches and Creatives

The Great Book of Journaling
(editor, with Lynda Monk)

Theoretical Alternatives to the
Psychiatric Model of Mental
Disorder Labeling (editor, with
Arnoldo Cantú and Chuck Ruby)

Transformational Journaling for
Coaches, Therapists and Clients
(editor, with Lynda Monk)

Fiction

Aster Lynn

The Black Narc

The Blackbirds of Mulhouse

Dismay

The Fretful Dancer

The Girl with the
Collaborator Sister

The Kingston Papers

Murder in Berlin

Settled

Meditation Decks

Everyday Calm

Everyday Creative

Everyday Smart

Programs

Creativity Coach
Certificate Program

Existential Wellness Coach
Certificate Program

CHOOSE YOUR LIFE PURPOSES

A Step-by-Step Guide
to Self-Awareness, Empowerment,
and Success

Debunking the Myth That You
Can Only Have One Life Purpose
When You Can Have Many

BY ERIC MAISEL, PHD

BOOKS THAT SAVE LIVES

MIAMI

For permission requests, please contact the publisher at:
Mango Publishing Group
5966 South Dixie Highway, Suite 300
Miami, FL 33143
info@mango.bz

For special orders, quantity sales, course adoptions and corporate sales, please email the publisher at sales@mango.bz. For trade and wholesale sales, please contact Ingram Publisher Services at customer.service@ingramcontent.com or +1.800.509.4887.

Choose Your Life Purposes: A Step-by-Step Guide to Self-Awareness, Empowerment, and Success

Library of Congress Cataloging-in-Publication number: 2024941532
ISBN: (p) 978-1-68481-606-4 (e) 978-1-68481-607-1
BISAC category code OCC014000, BODY, MIND & SPIRIT / New Thought

For Ann, forty-seven years into this adventure

Contents

A Few Words at the Beginning ...16

1. Not a Puppet, Not a Robot......17

2. Boom!......19

3. Even More of Nothing......21

4. Boys Sword Fighting......23

5. One Thumb Up......25

6. Evaluating Life Harshly......27

7. Formed Personality......29

8. Kittens, Puppies, and You......31

9. Thank Goodness!......33

10. Can a Bostonian Ever Leave Boston?......36

11. Energy Wisdom......38

12. Crouching Tiger......40

13. The Flip Side......42

14. Individuality......44

15. A Row of Tanks......46

16. Suppression......48

17. A Bright Light, A Step to the Side......50

18. The Study of Knots......52

19. Attaching/Detaching......54

20. Ethics and the Selfish Gene......56

21. The Humanistic Tangle......58

22. Values......60

23. And the World......63

24. The World and Sorrow......65

25. One Teenager......67

26. Mystery......69

27. Interlude......72

28. As If It Were Step-by-Step......74

29. On Broadway......77

30. Always Troubled......79

31. Three Lists......81

32. Huddled in a Bunker......84

33. Brick Walls and Rollercoasters......87

34. First Choosing......90

35. Classic Life Purpose Choices......93

36. Classic Choices: Excellence and Achievement......96

37. Classic Choices: Experimentation......99

38. Classic Choices: Self-Actualization......102

39. Classic Choices: Pleasure and Contentment......105

40. Classic Choices: Service and Stewardship......108

41. Classic Choices: Activism and Rebellion......111

42. Classic Choices: Appreciation and Gratitude......114

43. Classic Choices: Ways of Being......117

44. Classic Choices: Ethical Action......120

45. Combining Life Purposes: Creativity and Activism................123

46. Second Choosing..............126

47. Challenge I: The Elephant in the Room................129

48. Challenge II: Many Too-Small Purposes............132

49. Challenge III: No Purposes at All................135

50. The Wrong Question..............138

51. When Meaning Vanishes.....141

52. The Double Whammy............144

53. Challenge IV: Strangely Important.................147

54. Challenge V: Formerly Important.................150

55. Challenge VI: Core Doubt.153

56. Value-Based Choosing.........155

57. Opening to New Choices....157

58. Third Choosing................160

59. How Exactly?......................163

60. A Curated Week...................165

61. Milestones Deep Dive.............168

62. Second Interlude.................171

63. Support I: Your Life Purposes Statement............................173

64. Support II: Your Life Purposes Icon.............................176

65. Support III: Your Life Purposes Mantra.........................179

66. Support IV: Your Life Purposes Journal................................181

67. Eight Practices.....................184

68. Moments of Joy.................187

69. Negotiating and Navigating Each Day................189

70. Changed Circumstances...192

71. Age and Stage.................195

72. Life, Surfing.....................198

73. Life, Chosen.....................201

Resources and Further Reading.......................203

An Invitation to Get in Touch With Me.................................206

About the Author............................207

A Few Words at the Beginning

It would be lovely to think that choosing your life purposes might prove a straightforward, step-by-step affair. But human nature and human entanglements make that impossible.

You do not choose your life purposes in a vacuum. You must operate in your particular circumstances, with your particular personality, obligated here and responsible there, tripped up by life and teased by all sorts of desires, dreams, and passing fancies. You have no choice in the matter!

So, I'm obliged to paint a bit of a picture of life before we get to how to make life purpose choices and how to live the life purpose choices you've made. I have to set the stage a bit, as it were. Let's begin by looking at who we are—and at why it's past time that we make the vital shift from an unwarranted belief in something called "the purpose of life" to the better, albeit bracing, idea that we each decide for ourselves what matters.

CHAPTER 1

NOT A PUPPET, NOT A ROBOT

et's imagine that you were a robot rolling off the assembly line, built by a robot master to serve that robot master. Well, then you would have a singular purpose. Your purpose would be to serve that master. Done. Nothing much more to say about your destiny.

If that robot master accidentally provided you with consciousness, which of course would be a huge mistake on his part, well, then you might balk, rebel, doubt, and so forth. But having been built to serve, you would probably still serve, albeit now while "depressed."

But all of that has nothing to do with you. Nothing whatsoever. There is no robot master who built you to live out some singular purpose. That is a shopworn idea, even if billions of people still believe it. Leave all thoughts of a robot master or a puppet master behind. This is a new day.

In whatever way that we have mysteriously arrived here—this species of ours, this world of ours, this universe of ours—we can finally entertain and accept the fundamental proposition that we have been left to our own devices. And that is not a tragedy!

It is not a tragedy! That is what existentialists call freedom. It is not the freedom to sidestep life, as if we could even sidestep wars, famines, and epidemics. It is not that sort of freedom. No one is free that way. But it is the freedom to decide what's important to us—to each of us individually. That is our freedom.

You might think, even with anguish, "Well, if there is no singular purpose to life, then nothing can be important." But how does a child's laughter suddenly become nothing just because there is no puppet master? How does adding value become nothing? How does loving? To turn them into nothing is a mistake—but one that is so easy to make!

Here, we will undo that mistake. Let us leave behind the notion that there is some singular, elusive, handed-down-from-on-high purpose to life and settle into the brave, empowering, and altogether right idea that you get to decide what's important to you. You get to choose your own life purposes.

How will you make those life purpose choices? How will you decide which are the activities and the states of being you deem most important to you? Well, first of all, they must be meaningful to you! You are the arbiter of your own life purposes.

Your culture may say, "Turn over your life to taking care of your aging parents, even if they were always mean to you." You get to decide if you agree. Your government may say, "Fight in this all-important war," but it's up to you to decide if you agree. You may; or you may not.

Even if you feel very pressured by others, you can still take a step to the side and think about how you want to react. That important step to the side, which allows you time and space to bring awareness to the situation, is a great habit to acquire.

CHAPTER 2

BOOM!

"Choosing your life purposes" can be the centerpiece of your new philosophy of life. A philosophy of life is an attempt at a comprehensive answer to the question, "How shall I live as a human being?" It means answering the big question. And if it did manage to do that, wouldn't that be lovely?

But do you even need a philosophy of life? That must be the first question. Can't you just wake up, brush your teeth, hop on the bus, go off to work, shuffle papers, come on home, and watch a show? Isn't life straightforward and easy like that?

Probably not. That doesn't sound like the right life for a creature like us, does it? Don't you require more from yourself than just going through the motions? When you go through the motions, doesn't life feel meaningless, empty, and disappointing? Therefore, a philosophy of life is needed.

The philosophy of life you decide on should paint a picture of the world as it is and should make suggestions that strike you as valuable and true. Past philosophies and religions have not done an excellent job on either score. An accurate philosophy of life should include a sense of history. How did we arrive at our current sense of cultivated meaninglessness?

Starting in the seventeenth century, we have experienced four hundred years of the celebration—and inflation—of the individual. Certain amazing ideas bloomed, and some even more amazing realities followed. We got individual rights! We made scientific and technological progress on all fronts. There we were, beating back disease and living long lives. A wild, strange euphoria arose: humanity mattered!

But disaster was brewing. Year after year, we pushed the curtain back further until we stood face-to-face with a reality so cold that the space between the stars seemed blazing hot by comparison. Science, unintentionally and without malice, knocked us down a peg.

And holocausts continued. People still starved. With nuclear weapons came our ability to extinguish the entire species in the blink of an eye. We humans, for all our supposed progress and grand enlightenment, dropped a huge peg in our own estimation.

The more that we announced that humankind mattered, the more that we saw that we really didn't. The better we understood that the dinosaurs could be extinguished by an asteroid strike, the better we understood our own individual fate.

We began to understand the power of microbes, and even as we worked hard to fight them, we came to comprehend that something invisible yet endlessly prevalent could end our personal journey on any given afternoon. Boom!

CHAPTER 3

EVEN MORE OF NOTHING

The more science taught us, the more we shrank in size—and shrank back in horror. You could build the largest particle accelerator the world had ever seen and recreate the Big Bang—and psychologically speaking, end up with only more of nothing. And this is where we are today. We had somehow wagered that well-stocked supermarkets and guaranteed elections would do the trick and protect us from the void. They haven't. This is what we must now face.

Here is the answer: while we are here, we have the self-obligation to act as if we matter, a mattering that includes acting ethically and putting the whole world on our shoulders. This is what existentialists call an "absurd conclusion." It is "absurd" to care about life when life doesn't care about us. But that is the right answer.

To accomplish this, you take as much control as possible of your own thoughts, attitudes, moods, behaviors, and your very orientation toward life, and you make use of the freedom you possess in the service of what's important to you. You attend to what is called "the project of your life."

You identify your life purposes and take responsibility for your life purpose choices. You deal with meaninglessness by making daily meaning investments and by seizing daily meaning opportunities. And you dismiss absurdity as true but irrelevant.

Like it or not, we have been forced into the role of steward and arbiter of our own life. Surely no one asked for that. Who wouldn't prefer an orgasm, a tidy income, a little selfishness, and another round of golf? Wouldn't you? But is that what you want?

So, we try. We can't escape our psychological subjectivity, as we are embedded inside of it. But we can wonder about our own motives, we can make guesses about our intentions, and we can speculate about where we may be fooling ourselves. We can reflect. Inside of our cocoon of psychological subjectivity, a cocoon that makes it hard to see clearly, we can aspire to self-awareness.

We choose our life purposes, and then we live them. This sounds obvious enough. If you knew what your life purposes were, surely you would want to then live them, yes? But even people who have a good sense of what their life purposes are have difficulty actualizing them in their day-to-day lives.

This is because tasks, chores, errands, and everything else are allowed to come first; because juggling multiple life purposes is difficult; and because living our life purposes requires rather more effort than, say, napping or turning on the television. But let us set the bar that high: we will live our life purposes!

CHAPTER 4

BOYS SWORD FIGHTING

The idea that you get to choose your life purposes can be the basis of a philosophy of life that will serve you beautifully. This philosophy has its roots in many soils, among them existentialism, stoicism, language analysis, deconstructive postmodernism, the philosophy of science, and social psychology. It has proud antecedents!

When you acquaint yourself with the difference between life purpose and life purposes, with the value of self-authorship and self-obligation, and with the other ideas I'm presenting, I think that you will find yourself calmed by your new understanding and clear about how to proceed with life.

You will have the experience of this life mattering—even if the universe is indifferent, even if life's obstacles are relentless and enduring, and even if your own personality is an obstacle. You will have what you may have been looking for your whole life: an actual philosophy of life. Excellent!

One Saturday morning, I am sitting and writing in a small neighborhood park in Paris. The park is full. On a nearby bench, a woman is angry with a man. He tries to mollify her. On the next bench there's a relaxed middle-aged couple who have no need to say anything. Outside the park's swinging gates, a woman holding an infant is begging. Around me, a dozen boys are sword fighting. This is our species. This is life: concrete, real, and various.

You have seen a lot of life already, and you can decide for yourself how life works. You probably already knew all about life when you were five or six, even as your head began to be filled with commercials on television, commercials at church, commercials at the family dinner table.

You probably knew it all back then. But then life confused you. That's what living does. Now you can stand up, clear-eyed and clearheaded, and embrace a grown-up philosophy of life. It is a philosophy of life that is short on wishful thinking about the beneficence of the universe, our chances in the afterlife, the goodness of our fellow man, or how easy it will be to fulfill our self-obligations. It is short on all those things—meaning that it is real.

Every day we decide what matters to us. Each day we figure out how to deal with life. Our life is our project, and we strive to rise to the occasion. This is an ambitious philosophy which demands that human beings try. It asks them to make use of the freedom they possess, look life in the eye, and stand tall as both an advocate for and an example of human dignity. That's you, yes?

Some believe that life relentlessly pairs tremendous ordinariness with tremendous difficulty. In the face of all that, human beings can nevertheless adopt an indomitable attitude. This is not really to most people's taste. It makes work for them; it pesters them to be moral; it demands that they articulate their life purposes and actually live them. That is a lot!

But it is also beautiful. It is a way of life that encourages the best in you. It matches the high-bar vision you have of yourself as an instrumental, creative, ethical person who thinks for themself and cares for the world. A philosophy of this sort may genuinely serve you. Wouldn't that be something?

CHAPTER 5

ONE THUMB UP

Here is the new way in a nutshell. When you wake up, you hear yourself say, "What are the important things?" Not "What do I have to get done?" or "What did I leave undone?" or "What's on the news?" or "Another miserable day!" Rather, you hear yourself say: "What are the important things?"

Those important things might include having that hard conversation with your son about his drinking, making a sharp political statement, or creating your online business. Every day, you tackle as many of these important things as you can. You organize your life around your life purposes. This may not be easy—but it is the way.

By living this way, you feel like you matter. The contemporary person has powerful reasons for believing that he or she doesn't matter. Let's reject that notion, the idea that simply because we may be the product of an indifferent universe, we shouldn't act as if we matter. We make a decision to matter in human terms, on our own terms.

We matter by living our life purposes, by acting ethically, and absurdly enough, by taking responsibility for keeping civilization afloat. That is a matter of self-obligation, ordered by no one and ratified by few, and the primary way that we make ourselves proud.

But is civilization really worth keeping afloat? In one sense, absolutely not. Keep authoritarian regimes afloat? Keep grubby big businesses afloat? Keep endlessly warring cultures afloat? Keep oppressive religious traditions afloat? No, certainly not.

On the other hand, civilization also represents the best of us. We can choose our life purposes while keeping our eye on civilization's positives and our own humanistic impulses. We do not need to hold our species in high esteem in order to recognize, respect, and celebrate our species at its best.

We live in a time when that stalwart phrase from the nineteenth century, "truth, beauty and goodness," has been shredded by the analytical knives of linguistic philosophy. Today, it is hard to utter that phrase with a straight face.

Yet we are obliged to circle back around to innocence and to stand up for goodness, even though we know that badness is often rewarded, even though we know that our values compete and clash, and even in the absence of absolute moral principles.

That is, we decide not to give up nor give in. Without quite realizing it, many people have given up on life. They've made the mental calculation that life has cheated them; that life isn't what it's cracked up to be and that it just isn't worthwhile. That conclusion leads to a particular chronic sadness, sometimes called existential despair.

That conclusion makes it hard to stick with things or to believe in your own efforts. Therefore, a life-affirming gesture is needed. It is needed maybe a hundred times a day, given the depth of this despair. What is that gesture? You make the conscious decision to give life a thumbs-up, even if you have ample reasons to come to a different, harsher conclusion. Let's do that right now. Shall we give life a thumbs-up?

CHAPTER 6

EVALUATING LIFE HARSHLY

How we evaluate life matters. We experience life against the backdrop of our evaluation of life. If that evaluation is negative, nothing has much of a chance of feeling positive. Isn't it possible depression may just be a persistent negative evaluation of life?

Why might you evaluate life that harshly? Maybe because you went unloved as a child. Maybe because you've spent a stupendous amount of your time just earning a living. Perhaps because you see immorality rewarded. So many possible reasons!

Maybe you had dreams that never materialized and goals that you never reached. Maybe you had expected more out of life—more from it, more from others, and more from yourself. This list is potentially extremely long, isn't it?

It is easy and maybe even at times inevitable to evaluate life as a cheat, perhaps easier and more reasonable than evaluating it as worthwhile. But how many unfortunate consequences flow from such a decision and such a negative evaluation!

A negative evaluation of this kind is only a bit of the bedrock reality upon which you get to build your intentional life. If you have made such a judgment about your existence, it's possible you've appraised life correctly. There will be pain, there will be death, and maybe you'll only get only 3 or 6 percent of what you want. Maybe that's true.

Now, adopting this philosophy of life, you can face the truth that you consider life a cheat and move on. Now you can say, "Well, it looks like

I've concluded that life has cheated me. Let me say that as clearly and as openly as I can and get on with the project of my life!"

Evaluate life harshly if you must. But leap right to the next step. Shout, "So be it! Here I am, and I refuse to throw in the towel. I intend to live my life in a principled way, doing one right thing after another, to the best of my ability. Boom!"

Even though you may have ample reasons to feel that life is a cheat, you must, for the sake of experiencing meaning, for the sake of your emotional well-being, and because of some core moral imperative, move past that negative evaluation. You announce, "Life may be a cheat, for which I have ample evidence. But despite being burdened with this absurd hand to play, I see a way to play it. I see what I can do today, and I see what I can do tomorrow, and I see how to live."

You now choose to counter your negative conclusions about life with a dedication to your life as project. You make this leap even though you've been harmed, even though you've been badly disappointed, even though you find life taxing and unrewarding. You leap. Boom!

CHAPTER 7

FORMED PERSONALITY

The next step should be easy. Having given life a thumbs-up, having ratified life, having recommitted to mattering, you just choose your life purposes and live them. Voila! Ah, if only. Unfortunately, the door to that next step may be locked and bolted. Among many other impediments, it may be blocked by your own formed personality.

We stiffen into the person that we now are. That's a reality of human nature. In the picture that I'm painting, let's call that "stiffening" your formed personality. Formed personality is rather like a cement block. It "makes you" say that thing you regret saying the instant you say it. It may bore you, confound you, and make change and free will seem impossible.

It does not surprise us when we meet an old acquaintance on the street and he is still himself. Indeed, if he was very different, we would be a little shocked. It does not surprise us that he is still talking about that great real estate investment he made twenty years ago or the time when he made a killing on that certain tech stock. That's Bob. Hello, Bob. Nice to see you again.

Our formed personality stands between us and any real opportunity we might have to make strong, reasoned, completely current life purpose choices. Won't any effort we attempt to make to choose life purposes for ourselves be certain to come from that same repetitive, stiff, unthinking place that so much of what we think and do comes from?

It takes what amounts to a major effort, one that on most days we are not equal to making, to not tell that same story, to not travel to work by the same route, to not have the same recurrent nightmare, to not hold that same grudge, to not have the same breakfast, and to not bad-mouth ourselves in the same, old ways.

How boring! How tedious! No wonder that we may feel bored, no matter how busy we are. Who wouldn't be bored doing the same thing for the millionth time and thinking the same thoughts for the millionth time? Who wouldn't want to recklessly do something, anything, just as long as it was different? Of course!

As culture stiffens us, we become afraid of how we'll look to our neighbors. Work environments stiffen us, and we hardly dare do anything but exactly what's demanded and required. Family stiffens us; we know not to say a word to Uncle Jack about his weight or a word about her unemployed daughter to Aunt Sylvia. We learn this, we know this, and in this way we stiffen.

Then we defensively protect our formed personality. We carefully prevent ourselves from really knowing how stiff we've become because that knowledge would prove embarrassing and disappointing. Did I really kowtow to the higher-ups at work and say nothing? Am I really in this marriage just because my friends would shun me for divorcing? I don't want to know any of that!

We stiffen, and then we protect our stiffened self from self-inquiry. Maybe we go to therapy—and still repeat ourselves! Maybe we brave a firewalking weekend—and then still repeat ourselves! Maybe we gain an insight—and have it flutter away on the next breeze. We expect a bear to want honey, and we expect Uncle Dave to tell that same old story. Anything else would amaze us!

Here is the calculation that so many people are making just out of conscious awareness. "Let me just remain in my stiffened, well-protected identity. Who has the time, energy, or wherewithal to change? Better a not very meaningful day than a forthright confrontation with myself. Who needs that? That doesn't sound like fun!"

CHAPTER 8

KITTENS, PUPPIES, AND YOU

I f formed personality was the end of the story, that would be the end of an individual's evolution. You might be as stuck in concrete as a buried mafioso. But personality is made up of three parts, with formed personality making up only one part of the three. There are two other parts, original personality and available personality. Let's tackle original personality next.

Think about who you already were at birth. You did not come into life a blank slate. Anyone who has come into contact with kittens, puppies, or infants knows this to be true. Someone who misses the fact that one kitten is temperamentally different from another kitten is just not looking. One litter of kittens is a small universe of varying temperaments!

Our original personality includes everything with which we come into the world: we arrive endowed with specific traits of our biology, heredity, consciousness, temperament, nervous system, intelligence, sensing apparatus, orientation, and readiness, particular to each individual.

Original personality is our complete natural inheritance and includes everything from our intelligence to our sexual orientation. Our life purpose choices likely flow from and connect to our original personality— and the reality that we can never know what that original personality really is produces a huge headline. It means that we will have to choose our life purposes half in the dark, making decisions based on our reasoning and our intuition, against a background of genuine mystery.

This really matters. It matters fundamentally. Won't it have lifelong consequences for little Jane if she was born sadder and wiser than little Johnny? She may feel a little miserable her whole life long, for no other reason than that she is playing out her instructions. Is it too much to call this a curse? At the very least, it is consequential!

If Jane had been a blank slate at birth, it would follow that she would have no sense of violating some built-in set of instructions. She would have no reason to feel she had somehow become a 'wrong' version of herself. But if she was born already exactly herself—as is the case—then she would likely notice when she was not being true to her inner nature, and experience pain, discomfort, and disappointment.

What an idea! This means that on any given day, we may be pulled by our original personality in ways that perplex, disturb, and even derail us. Some sudden urge from our original personality may arise in us; some odd pain may return; some inexplicable thought from long ago—even from the beginning of the species—may turn us upside down.

Don't expect that old Aunt Estelle can answer the question, "Who am I really?" Maybe she can relate cute anecdotes about how charming you were at the age of two—but that won't amount to an answer. No test at the back of a magazine will do it, either. Maybe the best astrologer in town has the answer? Or maybe we'll just have to surrender, as we'll likely have to surrender many times over, to not knowing.

CHAPTER 9

THANK GOODNESS!

I s there a key to unlock those two doors, the doors of formed personality and original personality? Well, not quite a key. A key is too much to ask. But there is your available personality. That is your remaining freedom, the freedom you have left after the mysterious pulls of original personality and the shackles of formed personality are taken into account. Thank goodness for that!

Available personality is your freedom. Think of it as existing in a quantity that can fluctuate. If you're in the throes of an addiction, you have precious little freedom available. Maybe you have just enough to attend one AA meeting and stand way in the back—way, way in the back. Maybe you have exactly and only that much available personality on tap for you at this split second.

But by attending that meeting, and by listening to what others share, and by hearing folks talk about surrender and serenity and "one day at a time" and "first things first" and the other messages that infiltrate your brain, maybe a small but real chunk of the concrete is chiseled off and you have become just a bit freer. A tiny degree of freedom which maybe makes attending a second meeting just a little bit easier.

This is very different from you seeking out life's purpose. This is you dealing with you. This is you saying, "I've got this measure of freedom. Is it a lot? Is it a little? I have no idea. But it is enough to have gotten me to this meeting. And maybe it is enough to keep me coming back." This is you not seeking but choosing. This is you being as free as you can be under those circumstances.

Remember that seeking the purpose of life carries with it a frightening implication: the belief that you are not free to decide about life. In that view, you are obliged to align yourself with a higher truth, one higher than your own. That lockstep alignment is often charmingly called divine guidance, ancient wisdom, spiritual enlightenment, etc. But it doesn't free, it obligates.

You do not need to be granted your freedom to have freedom. Freedom need not come as some sort of gift or permission. You have your measure of freedom right now—within what is described here as your available personality—and you can have even more freedom as you liberate yourself from the shackles of your formed personality. Your original personality and your formed personality are constraints that may limit your freedom; however, they do not banish it.

It may interest you to think back and consider when more of your personality was available to you as well as when you had less of it available. What were the conditions and circumstances? Did you feel unfree at school and free while traveling? Unfree in your first marriage but much freer in your second? Unfree in groups and much freer when you acted independently? Take a peek back. What do you see?

Your available personality is something to cultivate. When you increase your freedom, when you make more of your inner resources available to you, that amounts to a personality upgrade. You become a better version of yourself. And wouldn't you love that better version of yourself to identify your life purposes? If so, then upgrading your personality might itself become one of your life purpose choices—and maybe one of the fundamental purposes!

Billions of words have been written about personality. All sorts of ideas have been floated. Attend one graduate program and you will think about personality one way; attend another graduate program and you will think about it another way. Each system of thought will have its own vocabulary, its own methodologies, and its own conceits.

The model of formed personality, original personality, and available personality that I'm presenting to you is just one more offering on the endless buffet line of personality theories. But maybe it makes some sense to you? I think it may. It takes into account our tendencies toward resistance as well as our originality and our freedom. Each of these will prove important to remember when you get to the actual task of choosing your life purposes.

CHAPTER 10

CAN A BOSTONIAN EVER LEAVE BOSTON?

Personality will likely prove an obstacle as you try to choose and live your life purposes. It is almost certain that identity will as well. Each of your self-identifications, except the gloriously large self-identification as a human being, amounts to a significant limitation.

Do you identify as Asian, a Bostonian, a woman, an activist, a mother, an American, a bohemian, an outsider? Each of these identities is an entanglement. Do your life purpose choices mesh with or clash with your identity as a Bostonian, as a woman, as an outsider, etc.? Clash or mesh? Mesh or clash? Such questions may torment you!

Are we hardwired to be French or Spanish? Are we hardwired to be a writer or a filmmaker? What funny ideas! But who knows? If we are, then aren't we going to feel miserable and somehow "off" not writing or not making films? If we try to choose life purposes that don't mesh with our hardwired identifications, aren't we going to feel as weird as we'd feel if we *tried* to choose life purposes at odds with our original personality?

And won't the identity you manifest at any particular moment be influenced, maybe dramatically, by your circumstances and by what's going on in the world? Won't your self-identification as Asian come to the forefront if you're the only Asian person in town, or if anti-Asian bias is suddenly in evidence due to an increase in hate crimes near where you live?

On any given day, are you reacting first as a woman first, or as a Methodist, or as an African American, or as a painter, or as a parent? And if today happens to be the day you choose your life purposes, won't the identity you're identifying with at that moment affect those choices? Imagine the difference between making life purpose choices as a mother versus making them as a painter!

And what if we are too attached to one of our self-identifications? What if we're clinging to our identity as a poet because we fear that we aren't really a poet, or clinging to our identity as an adventurer because not adventuring brings with it a whiff of meaninglessness? Making choices from those self-identifications may unwittingly send us on some great misadventures.

Won't it help if we can center ourselves on a strong, overarching identity as a human being? Different from and apart from all of our individual self-identifications, can we cultivate a large, integrated self that serves as our inner executive while remaining both separate from and larger than any particular self-identification? A central identity that isn't hooked on being a Methodist, a poet, or a Bostonian?

It's likely that we need our primary identity to be that of "human being" rather than Methodist, painter, Bostonian, woman, and so on. It is as that complete person that we know best what we value. To make a small joke of it, if you let the Bostonian in you decide where you will live, that means that you have no chance of ever leaving Boston.

It would be lovely if you made your life purpose choices as a whole person rather than from just one or another of these aspects with which you identify. To get the best results, choose your life purposes from your entire self, not only as a Bostonian, mother, or Methodist.

CHAPTER 11

ENERGY WISDOM

What is driving all of this? Life itself. Life is different from not-life. Our species is animated; it is alive. It is full of that driving force, human energy. We can't move on to choosing our life purposes without spending a moment on what animates us. Can you imagine a lifeless entity choosing its life purposes? How silly! It matters that we are energized, and how that energy uniquely expresses itself: it may cause us to race, to act impulsively, to get distracted, and/or to find kilowatts of energy for what interests us—or run out of steam entirely when required to deal with life's boring aspects.

Life requires energy, living generates energy, and life also steals energy. When inspired by a sudden passion, we are full of energy; encountering a sudden defeat, the energy drains right out of us. This is nothing like the simple mechanics of a toy stopping when its battery dies!

Human energy is no simple affair. Say that you crave more passion in your life. You decide to throw yourself into a creative project. Your energy soars! But then, you suddenly have trouble sleeping or relaxing. Was turning yourself on really such a good idea? Was it?

Well, you wanted the passion. But not all those consequences! Imagine racing down the road in a convertible with the top down and the wind whipping your hair. Lovely! But what if you are going too fast to negotiate that bend in the road? There you go, flying off a cliff!

We must become wiser about human energy. We need to understand what steals it, what creates it, when it is safe to increase it, what to do if our blood is boiling, and what to do if our energy has vanished. We need to understand all of its peculiarities and subtleties, because living our life purposes means managing human energy.

Nothing is more fundamental to human life than energy. But we have few good ways of speaking about energy. When it comes to electricity, we can talk about joules, watts and amperes. But when it comes to humans, we stand tongue-tied.

This lack of an energy language prevents us from taking a fundamental feature of human existence into account. Imagine chatting about the relationships among celestial objects without a notion of gravity. What nonsense would ensue!

Indeed, we are rather talking nonsense when we fail to credit the extent to which states like passion, obsession, compulsion, and mania, on the one hand, and boredom, listlessness, mental fatigue, and despair, on the other hand, are energy states.

We don't even know if we are for energy or against it! When we say that a child has high energy, aren't we making an accusation that something is wrong? We claim that his antics amount to a "mental disorder." His high energy is at best a terrible inconvenience. Wouldn't parents snap up a device that would drain away all that energy? Then what would you have? A lethargic child with "pediatric depression."

When you despair, your energy dissipates. Where did your energy go? You had all sorts of energy, and then you didn't. How can a mental state like boredom or despair possibly drain the body of physical energy? But it does. You might think that this subject is incidental to our discussion, but consider: will it make sense to talk about living your life purposes if we haven't factored in how energy comes and goes?

CHAPTER 12

CROUCHING TIGER

All that human energy! Sometimes it feels like the following: You heat up water in a boiler, which creates steam. You give the boiler no way to release that steam, so the boiler explodes. We do not want that!

Consider intensity. Intensity is a high energy state where our energy is all potentiality and where it is doled out very carefully, in the service of an intention. That tremendous energy is gathered and then, at some point, expended, perhaps explosively.

A sprinter is at the starting line. All that energy is gathered and held in readiness. The starting gun is fired. Off he goes! He was intense to begin with, but he kept all that energy in check. He is intense now, still, and finally expending that energy. Think about that sequence.

You intend to live your life purposes. You've made that decision. Not only that, but you intend to live them intensely. Feel that intensity, that energy? Where is it coming from? From your brain? Your heart? Your intentions? Your desire? Whatever its source, you are generating it.

A tennis player is about to serve. All of her energy is gathered and focused. But she tosses the ball into the air very carefully, even gently. That toss isn't where she uses all that stored energy. If she did, she would throw it a mile high!

Even with all that focused energy and all that high intensity, that tennis player can still do a careful, controlled, calm thing. That is quite a feat, when you think about it; all that energy pulsing through your body, and still you can toss a ball calmly into the air.

Someone with the passion, intensity, and wildness of a Winston Churchill could still sit quietly and paint. It is no contradiction or paradox that a creature with a ton of energy can also be the stillest of creatures. Picture a tiger crouching. Soon she will be all energy!

Right now, the tiger is in perfect stillness. She is still because she has her reasons. It isn't an abstract matter for her about "balancing energy with stillness." She is still so that the antelope doesn't see her or hear her. She is that still so that she can have some dinner!

We, too, even if we have kilowatts of energy at our disposal—even if we are bottled intensity itself—must know how to be still and stay still, not as an abstract matter, not for the sake of some abstract idea called balance, but because we can't live our life purposes if we are bouncing off the walls.

Imagine that you feel a ton of energy in your being, but your job is to sit still and write your novel or compose your symphony. It can be done; control and calmness are possible. But isn't all that pulsating energy a real challenge? Aren't you being pulled to explode? Watch out!

CHAPTER 13

THE FLIP SIDE

Can you feel how that pulsating energy almost cries out for a distraction, almost demands that you jump up and expend some of that energy? How can you write your novel if you are on the verge of an explosion? Doesn't choosing and living your life purposes demand amazing energy management?

But what about the flip side? What if you have too little energy? Isn't that what millions upon millions of people experience? Where did their energy go? Is it a matter of natural endowment? Medical issues? Difficult circumstances? Formed personality? Or something else entirely?

Well, we know some things. Do we experience more energy when life feels meaningful or when life feels meaningless? You know perfectly well that the experience of meaninglessness is an energy drain. But how can that be? How are meaning and energy related?

Consider: A neglected baby will first react energetically to her plight by crying and crying. But if she continues to be ignored, she will begin to lose her energy until she is practically inert. We call that terrible human phenomenon "failure to thrive." In this deeply demoralized state, she may even die.

Think about that. Maybe a given person's low energy is a direct result of her demoralization? Like a neglected infant who has failed to thrive, maybe she, too, is not thriving. No doctor can help her. She needs a revitalized life. She may need a revitalized life even to be able to begin to think about her life purpose choices!

Human challenges can reduce human energy, including becoming sick, demoralized, bored, or consumed by regret. Oppressive experiences of subjugation such as forced marches diminish human energy. Our energy supply is held hostage to our experiences of life. There you are in a thankless job; how energetic are you going to feel?

And what we are thinking matters. There is a direct relationship between what is going on in our mind and our energy supply. Even the most innocent thought can rob us of energy. We have an idle passing thought about the lawn needing mowing—and suddenly we feel exhausted!

Energy can drain away, just like that. And energy can also get hooked. We may have all this energy, but instead of marshaling it, we might turn it over to a worry, a fear, a craving, or maybe to some obsession with the latest video game or television series.

Our energy can and does get hooked, squandered, and stolen. Think of obsession, that high energy state where our energy gets hooked on a worry. Consider the peculiar high energy state called mania, where we mismanage a million kilowatts of our energy. What creatures we are!

Decisions about life purpose demand energy. What if our life force has been lost? What if we are squandering it on a big worry? What if we have constitutionally low energy as a feature of our original personality? You can see why we spent time here. High energy is one challenge; low energy is another. Let us pay attention to this strange thing with no real name!

CHAPTER 14

INDIVIDUALITY

We are approaching our main subject, how to choose and live your life purposes. We've taken a peek at how personality will involve itself in the process, as well as identity and energy. Next comes another one of those gigantic human issues: individuality.

When you were born, did you say, "Let me be like everybody else"? Did you say, "Let me be nobody in particular"? Or did you say, "Let me be me." Wasn't it the latter? Weren't you born to prize your own being? Wasn't that a feature of your original personality? That esteem is called individuality, and what mayhem it produces!

Let's picture one version of popping out of the womb. Looking around you, mistrusting all the rule-makers, feeling alienated and like a "stranger in a strange land," you find yourself burdened right from the beginning of your life by one pulsating inner demand: the demand that you be your own self.

That fierce need produces lifelong consequences. Maybe you find yourself presented with some odd-sounding rule—say, that God will be offended if you don't wear a hat. You find yourself obliged to ask, "Why?" And they will certainly tell you why!

The whole world will tell you why. But their answers likely won't make sense to you. So, you'll get your ears boxed or worse. You'll fall silent; or maybe you'll cry out, "No, I can't believe this nonsense!" Maybe you'll unwillingly acquiesce, or maybe you'll grow to be deeply oppositional.

If you take the oppositional route, you'll adamantly reject cookie-cutter answers that don't fit reality and instead try to make personal sense of the world. What will this feel like? It will feel like sorrow, anger, anxiety, alienation, rootlessness, and fierceness, all balled up together.

This oppositional attitude, maybe necessarily suppressed in childhood, likely begins to announce and assert itself in adolescence, and grows as an individual's interactions with the conventional world increase. A battle begins with all sorts of skirmishes.

This oppositional energy likely grows as your ability to "do your thing" is directly or indirectly restricted by the machinery of society. You find yourself in an odd kind of fight, not necessarily with any particular person or any particular group, but with just about everyone, possibly including yourself.

You may find yourself in a fierce battle with everything meant to constrain you and reduce you to a cipher. Any instance can be an occasion for this battle to be joined; when you encounter a falsehood or a nonsensical rule or restriction, a skirmish can be the repeated result. There you are, jousting with windmills while wriggling like fish bait caught on the end of a hook.

Maybe you'll rush headlong like a ski jumper down a steep ramp toward reckless ways of dealing with your feelings of alienation and frustration. Driven to be individual, there you are racing through life, not wisely, but fiercely and obsessively. That is one way this scenario can play out.

CHAPTER 15

A ROW OF TANKS

Born as an individual with a need to be yourself, you likely have more energy, more charisma, bigger appetites, stronger needs, greater passion, and more aliveness than the next person. Nature saw to this, blindly of course. It plopped unconventional you into an oh-so-conventional universe. What a funny joke!

Let me bestow all of this on you, nature itself jokes—here are some blessings: energy, desire, appetite, and much more! Of course, nature can't joke or bestow blessings. But nature desperately needs its avowed individuals, for the sake of the species! So, it produces you. And this extra energy and greater appetite and all the rest may be likely to incline you toward addiction, mania, and insatiability.

How could such supercharging not lead there? How can you have a ton of energy and not court mania? How can you have that much extra adrenaline and not want to drive a hundred miles an hour? Nature inadvertently created a fiery, insatiable creature. Nature does not joke; but it does produce unintended consequences. It made you fierce in this way, and it may have made it hard for you to ever feel satisfied.

You can eat a whole bag of peanuts and it might not be satisfying enough. It's also possible that you could write a good book or win a Nobel Prize and not find it satisfying enough. This inability to be satisfied can produce constant background agitation and unhappiness for those suffering from it. It also provides extra ambition and adds a susceptibility to grandiosity. As it bestows more powerful appetites, it can also add a susceptibility to compulsion. How charming of nature!

So, nature, which doesn't joke, nevertheless has its little joke. It creates an individual who must know for himself, follow his own path, and be himself. It then heightens his anxiety and makes sure that nothing will ever satisfy him. Good one, nature!

Your hunger for individuality is no unmixed blessing. But it is nevertheless a moral and psychological imperative. You can't both do right and be quiet. You can't both unleash your imagination and conform. You accept that you must be the individual that you must be. So be it!

Individuality is not a cheerful game or a stroll through the park. It is a tight-fitting suit that nature has fitted you with, making every step of the way half-uncomfortable. No need to thank nature for that!

This mandate to individuality can be a lifelong burden. In response, you might exclaim, "I didn't ask for this added pressure! But I accept it, since I refuse to live small or to shut my eyes."

Choose the rough road of self-obligation, self-authorship, and self-expression. Choose the rough road of radical independence. You must stand up because you know that you must, even though the results will likely be much less gorgeous than you might have hoped for.

Still, a lone individual can stand up to a row of tanks with the whole world watching. The tanks will win; but that image of defiance will be seared into the brains of a generation and may prove pivotal and even monumental fifty years later, when other tanks are gathering. That is something.

CHAPTER 16

SUPPRESSION

This sounds dangerous, doesn't it? It's possible you've known all along that the path of radical individuality is dangerous. So, maybe you've tried to suppress all that and blend in? How has that worked for you? Perhaps that effort has led to the state called "depression." That's where hundreds of millions of people have landed.

Suppressed individuality, rather than radical individuality, is the more usual path. A person is born individual but succumbs to conformity. Life then feels not quite right or worse—perhaps much, much worse. But something like a decision has been made, maybe just out of conscious awareness: being me is just too darn dangerous.

How well will life purpose choosing work if you have landed here? Imagine trying to decide on your life purposes while suppressing your individuality! What a strange tug-of-war that is bound to produce! What monumental existential anxiety ensues as you teeter between not mattering and mattering. Won't you fall in the direction of safety?

Maybe because of that anxiety you will simply avoid making the effort. That's entirely possible. You'll get to a certain point and feel too wobbly to continue. It's possible you've come to that point in life in all sorts of small ways, when you gave up practicing the violin or gave up on losing those extra fifty pounds. You silently said, "The heck with it!" and stopped.

The universe has no way to reduce that anxiety. By its starkness and relentlessness, it rather tends to increase it. It bakes that anxiety into your formed personality, making you exactly this uncertain of yourself. So, you will need to bring the calmness, as a gift from your available personality. "Here, self," you say. "It's safe to continue."

Whether you've been raging along, battling to remain individual, or traveling meekly while suppressing your individuality, you will now need to bring a new measure of calmness to your life, a deep breath of centeredness, so that you can make these life-affirming, life-challenging, life management decisions with calm, settled intensity.

Maybe your personal edge is grandiosity and arrogance; maybe it's meekness and passivity. Or perhaps it's both at once, a very typical outcome! I've dubbed that outcome the 'god-bug syndrome,' where you feel both inflated and deflated, bigger than life and smaller than a pea, the greatest composer ever but incapable of writing a note. Maybe that's where you've landed!

Or maybe you've landed somewhere else. Wherever you have landed, you'll likely require a process of uncoiling and unwinding. There are the challenges that come with suppressing your individuality and the challenges that come with expressing your individuality, and all of that has produced this rough you. So be it. Boom!

These tensions play themselves out everywhere in your system, in the way that you don't go out at night, in how you respond to what your sister says, even in your temptation to hide your boss's coffee creamer. They produce tremors, nightmares, misadventures, heroic stands, and embarrassing retreats. So, it is time to get ready.

These dynamics play themselves out most prominently in how and what you think and where your mind gets entangled. Let's spend a brief moment on mind and a few additional moments on the psychological entanglements that mind produces. We get so entangled! We surely don't want to choose our life purpose while ensnared in those same old ways, do we?

CHAPTER 17

A BRIGHT LIGHT, A STEP TO THE SIDE

We can't leave mind out of this discussion, even though it is a subject scaled for entire libraries rather than paragraphs. Let's give it just the briefest of glancing blows. We'll begin with the metaphor that you do your thinking in "the room that is your mind." In there, you have complicated conversations of which you may not even be aware.

All kinds of thoughts tumble around in there and come out the other side, typically as simple-sounding conclusions. For example, a simple-sounding thought like "This café is crowded" is likely the culmination of a complicated internal conversation about which you may be only half-aware. Many thoughts are like that.

Say that the thought "This café is crowded" is thought by a would-be writer who is struggling to write his novel and doubting his own ability to write it, and who most of the time finds excuses and reasons not to write his novel.

For him, the thought "This café is crowded" is not really an objective appraisal of the café. Rather, it is an excuse to not sit down and write. He thinks that thought, refuses to examine it, and feels justified in departing instantly.

When he gets to the next café, the thought that arises might be "This café is noisy," which will have arisen for exactly the same reasons. When he gets to the third café, the thought might be, "Oh, I know too many people here!" Again, he leaves right away.

Soon, he may find himself drinking Scotch instead of working on his novel; or hunting for sex, or finding a buffet, or starting a fight, or staring blankly out at the sea. By the end of such a disappointing day, isn't he likely to be filled to the brim with fury and despair?

Each of those thoughts about the cafés along his route sounded plausible enough: too busy, too noisy, too filled with familiar faces. But they were actually thoughts weaponized by the thinker against himself. They weren't innocent thoughts at all.

That is how our mind works. And if it is working like that, how will that affect—and maybe defeat—your life purpose decision? It would have served that would-be writer much better to not reflexively accept those thoughts as gospel, but rather work to ferret out their real significance and his underlying reasons for fleeing one café after another.

We wish he'd stepped to one side and reflected! You will want to take that step to the side as you choose your life purposes. You will want to settle on them with a light on, not in the darkness. Let's get a clear picture in mind of this simple-to-say two-step process.

You have a familiar thought; maybe it's an all-too-familiar thought, one that feels just a little bit suspect. The new and upgraded you knows to take a step to the side to pause and reflect. Simultaneously you turn on a bright light in the room that is your mind so as to see what's going on. There you go! No more rushing and no more darkness!

CHAPTER 18

THE STUDY OF KNOTS

The field of psychology ought to be conceptualized as the investigation of psychological entanglements—the study of knots, as it were. Maybe you are still tangled up with the way you read disappointment in your father's glance at that kids' piano recital thirty years ago. Something is still stuck there, all knotted and tangled. Knots!

You go to war, where you have terrible experiences, and you come home seriously troubled. Is it useful to say, "You have PTSD"? Or is it better to say, son, you are all tangled up, it looks like you're unable to leave those horrors and that guilt behind—there are some serious knots in place there.

What is an obsessive thought? An entanglement. It's a thing with claws, and it's got its claws in you! What is despair? Another entanglement. That level of sadness is a straitjacket, topped with chains. What is that raging inner dispute, that revenge fantasy, that self-pestering pattern, that silent reproach? It's just one entanglement after another!

Self-image is an entanglement. Maybe you're all tangled up with the need to look good—no, not good, perfect! You do something that reflects poorly on you—you drop the ball. Too tangled up with your self-image to tell the truth, you blame the weather, the wind, and how the sun got in your eyes. Knots!

Identity is another entanglement. You are born into a Baptist family. You identify with everything Baptist and get tangled up with everything Baptist. Every verse of scripture is another entanglement! For instance, there is the verse that says that you must be fruitful and multiply, apparently regardless of your individual inclination or situation.

We end up buying into so many identities in life: Wife-who-must-produce-babies. Less-favored-younger-sister. Devoted-daughter-who-must-sacrifice. Stiff-lipped-representative-of-the-upper-classes. Never-amount-to-anything-drunk. Must-be-a-dancer-at-all-costs. Entanglements!

Anything can entangle us; one glimpse of something, and we may be entangled for life. Maybe it's the atmosphere of a night café, the look on a stranger's face, or the shifting of a storm-tossed sky. It's as if even the idlest of experiences can come with crazy glue, leaving us stuck for a lifetime!

Think of what it's like to have a knot in your hair that can't be untangled without some discomfort. To unknot it guarantees pain! Is life like that? Are we guaranteed pain with each unknotting? What if we untangled from everything? Where would we be then? Free? Or perfectly unmotivated and in a state of despair?

Nature has created a creature who must stay motivated in order to stay alive. Without motivation, we would stay in bed and starve to death. How can nature keep us motivated? Build in hooks—all sorts of hooks. Hook us so fiercely that we are obliged to pay attention. Another one of nature's interesting tactics! Idly knot us up so that we don't slumber away our existence.

Of course, it goes without saying that this knotting affects our choosing our life purposes. Are we free to choose if we are also knotted and entangled? No, we are only free to a certain degree. We are only as free as we are. In that spirit, we take a step to the side, we turn on a bright light, and we do the best that we can, all entangled though we may be.

CHAPTER 19

ATTACHING/DETACHING

We may find that we're not quite certain whether or not these knots and entanglements may prove valuable. If this is nature's way, then we may want to be careful. To completely rid ourselves of entanglements might be to accidentally rid ourselves of motivation.

Perfect disentanglement might mean zero energy, zero passion, zero curiosity, and zero motivation. Without hooks to motivate us, what would life feel like?

Maybe the better goal, rather than to completely disentangle, is to accept the motivational value of entanglements, and then to create our own "mindful entanglements." There's a valuable exercise worth an afternoon: entanglements of our own choosing!

We certainly want permission from ourselves to carefully disentangle. We want permission to skip that family Thanksgiving dinner if it will only bring us grief, and the freedom to skip choosing a career just because something glittered or caught our fancy. We certainly want that freedom.

Another way to conceptualize this dance of mindful entangling and mindful disentangling is that we both attach and detach. We can invest in life: that is attachment. We can also unhook where we do not want to invest, i.e., mindful detachment. What a good pair of goals!

You step to the side and bring awareness to the situation. Is this a place to disentangle, notwithstanding the pain that will likely come with disentangling? Is this a place to remain entangled, despite the risks involved in staying with the status quo? Or is it the place to risk a new entanglement? You take a step to the side and consider.

Maybe you try to step to the side of your rocky marriage, to see it for what it is. But pain courses through as you try: the pain of failure, regret, and embarrassment. You can hardly manage that sidestep, so much pain is your effort generating. That step to the side is not easy!

However, the logic and language of this may prove comforting. If you feel that you have "depression," that may cry out for a chemical response. But what if you were to say, "I think I'm all tangled up in sadness." Isn't that very different? Doesn't a way out immediately suggest itself; namely, disentangling?

You might then nod and murmur, "Oh. It isn't that I am this thing called 'depressed.' It's that I'm being made sad by the way my mind has entangled me. If I could free myself of these entanglements, I might not be 'sad' at all. How interesting!" And so you dance the eloquent dance of attachment and detachment.

Your life purpose choices will amount to entanglements. Every choice entangles us. Our objective is not to shed ourselves of all entanglements, a move that might well leave us inert. Our objective is to wisely notice the quality and nature of our entanglements, and to try to unknot ourselves where the knots do not serve.

CHAPTER 20

ETHICS AND THE SELFISH GENE

We haven't yet broached a subject as important as any that we'll discuss: namely, ethics. To say that our goal is to identify what's important to us and then to live in the light of the choices we make means that we have to do a bit of thinking about what "important" signifies. Mustn't it sometimes mean "what's ethical to do"? And how will that work, given how frankly selfish we are?

I clearly remember an incident from second grade. I'd been out sick for a few days, and so had a classmate of mine. When we got back, our teacher informed us that she'd handed out a new reader during our absence. She sent me to the book closet to get our copies. In the closet were the two remaining readers, one in perfect condition and the other a bit shopworn.

I knew what was coming. I was going to have to hand one to the girl and keep one for myself. What would I do? I chose the better one for myself. I'm sure I had some excellent rationale for my choice. But I knew exactly what I was doing and exactly what I had done. I could therefore take no pleasure in having the better reader, because I knew I had acted selfishly.

Was this an earthshaking moment in the history of humankind? No. But it is telling that I remember it. Somewhere in your being you remember all those moments, too. You could have been generous, but instead you were selfish. You know. Of course, you had your reasons. Maybe they were excellent reasons, but likely they weren't. Likely you were just being selfish.

We are born self-interested. This must be true of every member of the species. But perhaps a percentage of the species is also born with a conscience and a humanistic impulse? Maybe that is the same kind of person who pops out of the womb stubbornly individualistic, the sort of person who appreciates the idea of naming her own life purposes? You, that is.

You are selfish, like anyone, and also better than that. Ah, but what mayhem such conflicting impulses produce! Mustn't a lifelong battle between selfishness and caring ensue? You want what you want. Who doesn't? At the same time, you know better. What a mad mix of grandiosity and altruism! Who can make sense of it?

There is a part of our nature that champions truth, beauty, and goodness. There is another part of our nature that wants its slice of the pie—the largest slice. There is a part of us that reveres ethical action. There is also a part of us that is pure trickster. If you were given a button to press that would destroy the world, would you press it? On most days, maybe not. But on that particularly bleak Tuesday?

Maybe you opt for the ethical thing. But let us not be seduced by the notion that it is bound to feel good. In fact, it may feel dangerous, or confrontational, or embarrassing; or consequential in some other way. Ethical action is like that. It's no wonder that our selfish genes rise up and announce, "Forget ethics! I'm more in the mood for a bubble bath!"

We understand this about ourselves. To remind ourselves of this reality, maybe we organize ourselves around the shining idea that we are going to do the next right thing. We intend to do so even if that thing isn't easy, even if that thing brings with it real consequences, even if we prefer a bubble bath or some trickster deviousness. That would be special.

Let's say that you do a wonderful job of tamping down your selfishness and affirming that humanistic impulse inside of you. Will you have landed at a secure place where the ground beneath you has stopped shaking? No, not likely. More likely, you've landed in a new briar patch, a place of new entanglements. Let's take a glance at why.

CHAPTER 21

THE HUMANISTIC TANGLE

Selfishness and the humanistic impulse do not stay at arm's length from each other. They get all tangled up! It is so devilishly hard to maintain the purity of that altruistic impulse! Do you want that residency, or do you want your friend to win it? Will you read your children a bedtime story when your own story is wanting to be written? Who is more entitled to stay home and paint, you or your spouse? Golly!

You are a medical researcher. You really want to find a cure for the disease you're studying. But when scientists on the other coast get to the cure first, you grow furious. They won! You forget all about the main point that there is now a cure.

You are a choreographer. Your upcoming dance is brilliant, except for that tired middle bit. You could lift a wonderful sequence from that show you just saw, but that would be stealing. Or would it? Well, yes! But maybe no. Darn it!

You are a poet. Your family needs more money. There is no way you can contribute to the household kitty except by taking on some life-sucking job that will kill your creative soul. What will you do, defend your right to create or toil away like some worker bee?

You are a great composer. You want to write a symphony in defense of freedom. That need is vibrating in your body. But the tyrant who runs your country is bound to retaliate and harm you and your family. Stand up? Or compose a jovial musical comedy?

You really want to write a cozy mystery series. But is light entertainment really of value? Is that how you're supposed to express your humanistic impulse, in such a trivial way? You go back and forth, back and forth, and can't settle enough to write anything. Cozy? Literature? Cozy? Literature? Darn it!

You run the philanthropic arm of a giant corporation. Your work is good and true. But you also know that your department is a public relations ploy meant to smooth over the fact that your corporation is a worldwide polluter. Can you happily continue?

You're an architect with a thousand ideas. But is what you want to do just all ego and excess? Does the world really need your outlandish creations? Or does it need more affordable housing? How can you justify spending hundreds of millions of dollars just to produce something new, iconic, and avant-garde?

What a mix of beauty and nonsense is fashion. What a mix of excellence and ridiculousness is fine dining. What a mix of celebration and excess is a fifty-million-dollar painting. What a mix of artistry and pandering is a blockbuster movie. These are the collisions that await us.

Of course, you can see why this had to be another one of our preliminaries. To ask yourself "What's really important to me?" is also to ask yourself to brace for all these inevitable encounters with your personality, facing your self-identifications, your inborn selfishness and egotism, and the tangled knots that desire and generosity create.

CHAPTER 22

VALUES

Naturally, we want our life purpose choices to be informed by our ethics. So, naturally, we want them to be "value based." This is another lovely idea that is so simple to say but so hard to make sense of in real life. Is taking a beautiful picture of a homeless person more valuable than taking him into our home? Hmm?

The existentialists were excellent at painting a clear picture of how easy it is to say "live life according to your values" and how hard that can be in reality. Values compete; values contradict one another; values shift. Here is one classic existential example. Your ailing mother needs your help or she will die. Your country needs you to fight a ferocious enemy invading your land. Which do you choose? How do you choose? And whichever you choose, won't you be left with a terrible taste in your mouth?

Is it really easy to know which values you want to uphold in a given situation? It is one thing to value compassion, discipline, freedom, and gratitude. Those are four fine and laudable values. But what will you do when the principal at the school where you teach begins to censor your class materials? Feel gratitude that you still have your job and that your principal didn't take even worse measures? Feel compassion for the pressures put on him? Decide that the way through this moment is by maintaining a disciplined attitude? Or fight for freedom by speaking up?

Any one of these decisions might be "value based" and might align with one of your values—but how different each reaction is! And will we even know what is motivating our choice? We can easily and defensively turn a desire into a value through rationalization or by employing some other defense mechanism. It is all too human to say that we are acting ethically when we are just reacting defensively!

Say that you opt for "compassion," a perfectly laudable value, and keep silent about the censorship, arguing internally that your principal is under a lot of pressure and that the compassionate action is to support him at this difficult moment. But won't you know in a corner of consciousness that you are not really practicing compassion but rather protecting your job and your way of life?

Or on the other hand, it is of course possible you may really not know that you've made a defensive decision, and you may argue long and loud that you're doing the ethical thing. It is an everyday feature of our species that, because we want to seem ethical, we will often call an action ethical even when we've chosen it for some rather more shadowy reason.

And what if the value that we are prioritizing no longer seems valuable to us? One day you may value beauty and decide that writing poetry is a prime life purpose choice. A year later, you may decide that poetry is "mere words" and that you value action more. Two years later, having worked a lot in the world, you may find yourself flooded by the feeling that poetry possesses far more value than the work you've been doing.

The "value" of poetry may shift countless times as you live your life. Similarly, so may the value of "career," "intimacy," or "health." Career may give way to tending your garden. Intimacy may give way to a devotional solitude. Health may recede to a back burner if you must do something that takes your focus away from your own well-being, like providing round-the-clock care for an aging parent suffering from Alzheimer's. This is life!

By all means, create your list of values. I will ask you to do that in a while. It will be lovely to know what you value. Maybe you can even rank and prioritize them, and land on your "top values." But remember that there is no way to directly apply that list to the task of life purpose choosing. At any given moment, that value list is bound to whirl like a spinning galaxy.

Picture values colliding like two asteroids slamming full force into one another. Care for your aging parents or have a life? Accompany your spouse halfway across the world or opt for your own career? Choose medicine or choose poetry? Say the kind thing, say the true thing, or say nothing? Boom!

CHAPTER 23

AND THE WORLD

So far, we've been inside you, chatting about your personality, your identity, your energy, and so forth. But there is an outside, too. We call that "outside" by various names: the world, culture, society, family, circumstances, and, in the language of existentialism, embeddedness and contingency.

Any philosophy of life worth its salt must also be a philosophy about the world. It must demand of itself that it address how society and culture operate, what forces align against the individual, and how each individual might want to relate to that messy, pressing reality. You may choose your life purposes while sitting on your easy chair, but you must live them in the world.

We are obliged to be real and true-to-life about our circumstances. Human beings are not free to ignore quarantines, market crashes, cruel parents, persecutions, earthquakes, industry closures, or eight-month winters. Our circumstances matter. Sometimes our circumstances support us. More often, they are hard on us.

That hardness demoralizes us and leaves us shaking our heads. What are we supposed to do about climate catastrophes, the reappearance of plagues, shameless greed, religious warfare, fender benders, and pimples appearing on the morning of prom night? Really, what are we supposed to do? Shut our eyes? How well will that work?

Well, we return to our first principles: we demand of ourselves that we make strong life purpose decisions and strive to live those life purpose choices, even as we're forced to take the world and all of its slings and arrows into account. That is, we try. We stand up, look our circumstances in the eye, and try.

Of course, we can't know beforehand if our efforts will work. We make our decisions based on our limited understanding of the world; and, far too often, we discover that we've gotten the picture wrong. What we tried didn't pan out, because our personality got in the way, because the work was just too hard to do, because the world was too obdurate and unyielding, or for one of a thousand other reasons.

The world is rather more our albatross than our oyster. As a child, you didn't quite know this. You heard homilies and learned the rules of your culture. You took in certain fairy tales: the ideas that if you tried, you would be bound to succeed, that good always wins in the end, and so on. Your whole culture was a kind of motivational speaker, cheering you on to buy a new car, win beautiful prizes, and let the sun shine in.

Yes, you got sold a bill of goods. Now, you accept the reality that the world is exactly what it is, and you make your life purpose choices unfettered, as much as is humanly possible, by myth and fantasy. Now, if you decide to write a novel, start a home business, save free speech, or help your children flourish, you know that will not be a walk in the park. The world is not a park.

Picture a wise seven-year-old. She has questions that she may not dare to ask. How can it be that millions of children are starving? Can't they be fed? Why are people homeless? Can't they be housed? Why do her parents pretend that a fat man is bringing her presents at Christmas?

If she does dare ask, what humbug will she be told? She sees the world clearly with her own two eyes—but it may take many years of living before she can process what she sees. It may take decades before she can say, "Oh, this is the world. I get it. It is exactly what I always knew it to be. Now, let me factor it into my calculations."

CHAPTER 24

THE WORLD AND SORROW

Because the world can be hard as nails, because our efforts to live our life purposes regularly fail, because we quickly learn about loss, injustice, impermanence, deception, and death, there is no help for us: sorrow will live between the lines of life.

You will experience sorrow. You are a human being, and all human beings experience sorrow. And since you are human, you'll experience sorrow at the oddest moments, even when life is good or when something excellent happens. We are built exactly this way, to feel sorrow even when life feels good, because we know that this good moment will pass and fade.

Life can be good. Life can be rich. Life can even exceed our expectations. But even at such moments, and often especially at such moments, feelings of sorrow, melancholy, and regret invade us. That a given moment can be at once wonderful and sorrowful speaks to the layered nature of now. Now is no simple thing. Nature built us to contemplate death even as we smile, kiss, and hug.

You hold your child's hand and experience a wonderful moment. Suddenly you're sorrowful. You're confronted by the inevitable passage of time and by the knowledge of all that your child will be obliged to experience in life, the bad with the good. You are invaded by the knowledge of the impermanence of life. This simple physical touch provokes that knowledge, and tears start flowing.

That is how "now" works. We know this. We know that painful thoughts and feelings are always hovering nearby, ready to drop down into the moment like acid rain. Sorrows don't live across town. They live just off to the side of every moment, waiting. We therefore choose our life purposes against the backdrop of this knowledge. We smile a small smile and exclaim, "Okay, now! Make me sad, if you must. I still intend to live."

We know that this sorrow is not "depression." It is the song of a world in mourning, mourning its very nature. There is something about love wrapped up with this sorrow, and something of compassion. Maybe sorrow is a teaching feeling. Why would nature do that? Maybe so that we live with our eyes wide open to mortality, urging us to live, now.

The pain of sorrow, which we do not crave and do not want, is maybe like the pain that tells us that our hand is too near the fire. Maybe it is crucial for our well-being. We do not love such reminders, but maybe we need that reminding. Holding our child's hand, feeling the pain of the moment as well as the joy of it, we are reminded of what we have and what we will lose. That experience of sorrow resets our compass. As a result, we spend the afternoon baking cookies.

Had we not felt that sorrow, we might have been inclined to do the laundry or clean up the living room. But because we got that whiff of mortality, we decided that baking cookies was our way to love. Sorrow invited love in, and we decided to love.

Sorrow is such a complicated feeling, because part of what we're experiencing is our love of life. We feel sorrow because we can love, because we have loved, and because we can still love. Maybe sorrow only comes to someone who still loves life?

As we make our life purpose choices, we can expect to be flooded with feelings. This sort of choosing is not like taking a multiple-choice test. It isn't an uneventful, unemotional, all-gray sort of thing. It is spiked, colorful, challenging, and bracing. It is bracing and embracing. We bring everything to it, our dreams, our hopes, and the sure knowledge that all this will pass. Be gentle.

CHAPTER 25

ONE TEENAGER

Picture a fifteen-year-old struggling with his world. His world is home, high school, the Internet, mass culture, texts, encroaching fascism, constant news, plus all those cataclysmic events that affect him: a rash of suicides, a rash of school shootings, a rash of expectations.

He is sorrowful. Call it despondent; call it melancholic; call it feeling down. What he is not is "depressed," if by that we mean that he is having a problem with his hormones, his genes, or his neurotransmitters. Both the wide world and his narrow personal world have made him despondent.

What should we invite him to do? How can we help him? We can take him fishing for the weekend or enlist him in a project to get his mind off the world. But most crucially, we can invite him to become a philosopher, to learn and absorb certain ideas even if he can't quite make use of them yet. But he can begin. He can already begin to live his life purposes.

We can paint him a picture of how to live in this world just the way it is, with its precise difficulties. We can help him understand why it is his obligation to stand up, to absurdly rebel against the facts of existence, to identify and then to live his life purpose choices. He can take that in. He can begin to picture navigating and negotiating each day in new ways.

He is just fifteen, of course. He will have a lot on his mind. Much of it will feel obsessive: pimples, video games, the girl who isn't giving him the time of day, the car he wants, the band he'd love to start, the way his grades aren't what they should be. He is at that stage of life, and he can't be elsewhere. But we can still advise him. We can still paint him sensible pictures.

He keeps his headphones on to drown out his parents' fights. In his peripheral vision, he sees that the polar icecaps have melted further. Then there is the teacher who has it in for him. And the pimples! And so much Spanish vocabulary homework! Live his life purposes? What a joke. Yet still...

Into this obsessive, claustrophobic, melancholy world we can drop hints about his obligations, his choices, and his path as an individual. Maybe these ideas will ring a bell with him, or maybe they won't. Either way, maybe we can pry him from his video games for a little while and invite him to think.

We invite him to think about the world. It is not an invitation he is usually offered. What he is usually offered are trailers for the blockbuster films coming at Christmas. We offer him something very different: a philosophy of life to chew on. Maybe we can prevent him from blindly seeking and spare him decades of looking and wandering. Perhaps we can help him to really understand the power of choosing.

The world is implacable. Sorrow is inevitable. That doesn't make life a strictly dark affair. But it does make it an enterprise crisscrossed by shadows. On some days those shadows will make for darkness. On other days, they will highlight the light. This is true for our fifteen-year-old; this is true for me; this is true for you.

During a sweet dream, we escape the world. How lovely a respite! There are the scents of flowers and the smiles of children. Wars end and waves of peace commence. But then we waken and the obdurate world returns, as it always does. We take that into account as best we can and make our choices.

CHAPTER 26

MYSTERY

We must make those choices against a backdrop of genuine mystery. Life is a mystery, indeed. But what do we mean by that word? What are we insinuating? Are we saying that there are angels in the attic? Or are we saying something very different, that what we can't know might prove very interesting...except that we can't know it?

A first sense of mystery is "a puzzle to be solved." Who killed the prince? Was it his third wife? Was it the butler? Maybe the killer will be captured, or maybe he or she or they won't. But there is nothing very startling or "mysterious" going on here. There is just some current not knowing. Probably we will know at some point and the killer will be arrested. Or maybe this mystery will never be solved. Either way, we do not find anything particularly mysterious about mysteries of this sort.

A second sense of mystery is "a pseudo-puzzle to be solved." In this instance, there is no real puzzle, just an ordinary something that happened. I thought I put my car keys down here. Oh, but look, they are way over there. How mysterious! No, not really. Neither of these senses of "mystery" concern us very much. Who killed the prince? How did our car keys get over there? A philosophy of life can safely stay silent on the art of detection and on everyday forgetfulness.

A third sense of mystery concerns things that look to be frankly unknowable—but unknowable in an obvious and trivial sense. We can't know if there were pancakes before the Big Bang or whether they came with syrup. There's not a chance we can know that. Such trivially unknowable "forever mysteries" are hardly troubling. The rational mind knows exactly why such mysteries are unknowable and moves on to other things.

Puzzle mysteries, pseudo-puzzle mysteries, and trivially unknowable mysteries hardly trouble us or get in the way of choosing our life purposes. They may be important to mystery writers and to astrophysicists, but they don't agitate us. But there is a "mystery divide" that does matter. It is the way that we get impaled on the fence of not knowing if life works one way or if life works another way.

Is it ridiculous to believe in premonitions? Is it ridiculous not to believe in premonitions? Why can't it all be clearer, exactly this or exactly that, and not some jagged fence to ride? For instance, we haven't spoken to a friend in ten years. We haven't thought about her in months. Today, we think about her. Ten minutes later we receive an email from her. Darn! What is that about?

Neither probability theory nor improbability theory are really convincing on this score. Yes, things that are a billion-to-one do happen. But are the odds actually a billion-to-one? Really? Besides, it didn't feel random. It felt very much like something else. If we do not believe in made-up gods, then we certainly do not want to let them in by some back door. We do not want to freight words like "mystical" or "spiritual" or "metaphysical" with an importance in which we don't believe. But it is hard to just smile.

A philosophy of life can't settle this mystery debate, close the mystery divide, or make believe that an answer is waiting in the wings. Even the wisest philosophy of life has no power to do any of that. It can, however, acknowledge the divide. We want resolution, relief, assurances, comfort, a coming together. We want answers. But maybe all we can have is an understanding that mystery is mystery.

Why is this important? Because life purpose choosing involves us in the most fundamental decisions, including about life and death. How are we to decide if we don't know the fundamentals? How are we not to doubt our own intentions when everything can be doubted? How can we bet everything on our own discernment when there might be some completely different wager with better odds?

Yes, this is another face of absurdity. Can a bridge be built that honors both stalwart rationality and metaphysical possibilities? It is hard to see how. Maybe this must be a place of grace and surrender. Or could it be a place of absurd rebellion, where we laugh in the face of mystery and stand up just a little bit taller?

CHAPTER 27

INTERLUDE

We do not want to do what the blind men do in the tale of the blind men and the elephant. We do not want to chat about personality, identity, mind, psychological entanglements, individuality, energy, and all the rest, and imagine that we have painted an accurate picture of us. No. We are the whole elephant! We are not the sum of any discussion.

So, let us shed the many observations leading up to this point. Let us ready ourselves for the next step, the step of choosing your life purposes. Let us get ready by letting go of previous discussion. Zen Buddhism presents the idea of letting go of all that we know for the sake of arriving at beginner's mind. Let us do that, too. Whoosh. We are free and beginning.

Let's be quiet for a moment. You've been in your skin for a very long time now. Unlike a snake, you can't just shed your skin. So, let us be quiet for a moment and be with that reality. In that silence, which I hope you can imagine if not actually inhabit, let us shed whatever we can in service of the new life I'm offering.

Maybe there is a heavy overcoat to remove. Maybe there are some dark sunglasses. A million pellets have come at you over the years, pockmarking your skin and making healing hard. Are there still some of those steel balls under your skin? Can they be popped out, with a nice little pop that breaks the silence?

I've never wanted to write a memoir. For one, it feels like it would be an invasion of the privacy of those around me. For another, I don't want you to know me that well. But there's a third reason, that memoir plays a fast and loose game by making believe that the inexplicable can be made explicable. It can't.

Let us be quiet for a moment. Isn't it inexplicable how many generations are lined up behind you? How will all those millions of choices, choices made ten thousand years ago or on a boat coming over from the old country, infiltrate your life purpose choosing? Consider that, in this moment of silence.

So, you will be doing something in a moment, choosing your life purposes. But you are also participating in thousands of years of life purpose decisions. Someone, somewhere, had to put up storm shutters in order to survive a tropical hurricane. Someone, somewhere, had to know not to eat those poisonous mushrooms. Take that in.

Maybe your life purpose choices will already want to shift a bit in this silence, in the light of all those eons. Maybe poetry suddenly makes more sense. Perhaps a pilgrimage to a place you never thought of visiting now feels right. Maybe giving a kind word to the child of yours you're fighting with is a coherent option. Look far back, before there were candles. Choices were made then. Choices must be made again.

Ready yourself for process, for genuine process.

Genuine process is never really step-by-step. Something comes to you in the middle of the night that changes everything. Your values shift. You overhear a conversation and change your mind about what's real, about what's important to you. Two ideas collide and give you a headache.

That is process. But we also have it in us to imagine what step-by-step process might look like. Let us go there, finally. Let us be quiet for another moment and then tie our shoelaces. Now comes a time for lists, for sorting, for all of that rationality. We will act for a while as if $2 + 2 = 4$, even if it actually equals 5.

CHAPTER 28

AS IF IT WERE STEP-BY-STEP

Let's presume for the moment that the effort to choose your life purposes allows for a step-by-step process. Maybe you start by considering what's really important to you at this moment in your life. Then you do the next thing and the thing after that. What might that path look like? It could be something like the following nine steps.

Step One: You decide; you decide that you and your efforts matter, that you want to live in accordance with your own values and principles, and that your life purposes are yours to name and frame. Step one involves making a certain decision and taking a particular stance. It is a bit like going to the gym—the existential gym. You grasp that bar, put the heavy weight of your life on your shoulders, and prepare for an overhead lift.

Step Two: You honor the nature of the task. You recognize that naming and framing your life purposes may prove at once impossibly complicated and also simple, as simple as coming up with a life purposes statement that you follow. Maybe you create a huge list of the values that matter to you and wonder what on earth to do with that long, contradictory list. You try to factor in your circumstances, your personality quirks, everything. How complicated! Or you might decide that "do the next right thing" nicely captures the essence of your life project. How simple! Complicated? Simple? Both?

Step Three: You announce what's important to you. In whatever fashion you get there, you distill your list and formulate what's important to you. Then you nod. "Yes, my health really is important to me." "Yes, my creativity is really important to me." "Yes, finding meaningful work is really important to me." "Yes, repairing my relationship with my children is really important to me." Etc.

Step Four: You restate those important things as life purpose choices. This is an easy step linguistically. You just say, "My health is one of my life purpose choices" instead of "My health is really important to me." Linguistically, it's that simple. But these restatements are psychologically crucial. To call something a life purpose choice is to anoint it, strengthen it, and commit to it.

Step Five: You elaborate on your life purposes choices, clarifying and refining them. You've announced that your health is a life purpose choice. But what does that mean? Is that primarily your physical health? Or your emotional health as well? Is that more about diet and exercise, or more about finally getting off that one medication with all its debilitating side effects? What exactly do you mean?

Step Six: You translate your life purpose choices into actions. Moving from "health" to "diet + exercise + meditation + medical check-up" is brilliant. Next, what will you actually do (and not do)? Have blueberries and yogurt for lunch every day? Stop eating at seven in the evening? Empty the cupboards of all processed snack foods? These are the mundane consequences of life purpose choosing!

Step Seven: You align your thoughts with your life purpose choices. You want to make a career change and find more meaningful work. That's a clear life purpose choice of yours. But how well can you proceed if you are thinking "I have no chance" and "All work is meaningless" and "It's too late for me" and "I have no real skills"? Do we agree that thoughts of this nature would not serve you all that well? Indeed, if those were your thoughts, would you even try?

Step Eight: You institute practices that support your life purpose choices. Writing a novel is one thing. Instituting a daily writing practice is a different thing—and the best way to honor your life purpose choice of writing. A writing day that produces twenty words is far better than a not-writing day filled with regrets about not writing.

Step Nine: You live your life purpose choices. We do not want to create a list that leads nowhere. This is meant to be a lived philosophy of life, not a lip service one. You live your life by organizing it around your life purpose choices. This isn't for next year, or for when the kitchen remodel gets done. This is for now—right now.

CHAPTER 29

ON BROADWAY

That was the step-by-step version. But human reality is different from that. Let's look at a few scenarios where people with real lives, a history, desires, regrets, complications, and all the rest engage with life purpose choosing. Imagine the following.

You've been an actor, and it hasn't worked all that well. You've had a few roles, a few commercials, a few student films. But that isn't much for a lifetime's work. What do you do now? Throw good money after bad and announce acting as one of your life purposes? Or is it time to change careers, switch identities, choose a completely new path? How hard!

Plus, you've gotten older. Is health, fitness, diet and all of that more important now? Does "health" need to get elevated to the level of being a life purpose choice? Who wants to think that much about diet and exercise! But...is it time? Is it time to raise health to a place of higher priority in your life?

Ah, and your marriage. It is...what's the right word for it? Stagnant. Twenty-five years with the same person, and much of it just okay—maybe a little less than okay. It exists, every minute of the day, but is it even important? Or is it just background noise? What to do there?

And then there's wanderlust. It's a form of restlessness, almost like some kind of itch. If you aren't careful, you might throw everything over and take yourself to Fiji. But what would that get you? Some tropical disease? What to do with this itch, this restlessness! How can all that be turned into a life purpose choice?

Then there are some very old dreams. Brilliant dancer. Great writer. One-woman show performed everywhere, on Broadway, in Berlin, at the best West End theater. And other dreams, dreams without names and without shape, that amount to painful longings.

There is also confusion; about mortality, about what's really important, about those not-very-nice aging parents of yours, about friendships that don't amount to much, about what those nightmares signify, about that persistent ache sometimes in one toe, sometimes in another, about...

What the heck does life purpose choosing even look like here? Should you reinvest in acting, or perhaps quit it entirely? Should you try to live quietly, dieting a little, having lunch with friends, and avoiding replying to your mother's dramatic texts? Or should you get a divorce, take a new lover, and rush off on an adventure?

Doesn't sound promising, does it? Yet that is exactly where you are. Forget about step-by-step. Forget about easy. Put on that one Irish sweater that makes you happy, go to a café, have a scone, empty your mind, and murmur, "Okay. Let's tackle this."

Where will this café hour take you? Will we see you in Fiji in the spring? Will we see you off-off-Broadway in your one-woman show eighteen months from now? You have this ball of yarn—unravel it. Be patient. Be brave. This is life purpose choosing in a nutshell. This is one scenario envisioning how you might do it.

CHAPTER 30

ALWAYS TROUBLED

Let's paint a second picture of life purpose choosing. If the following doesn't match your own life, try out imagining that these are your circumstances as a thought experiment for the length of the next couple pages. You have always been troubled, although not troubled as in incapacitated; in fact, you've done plenty of exemplary things in life. You've worked in the business world and made money. You've volunteered and run events. You've raised children. That you have always been troubled doesn't mean that you haven't played the game of life. But you have always been troubled.

Haven't you been a lot more anxious than you would have liked? Haven't you receive a diagnosis of depression? Haven't you been reckless and self-destructive? Haven't you found yourself on a roller coaster with your weight? Haven't you lost hours down this or that rabbit hole? Haven't you been living too dangerously and too unhappily? Haven't you hungered for a sense of purpose?

You may have no trouble making lists. If told to list "what's important to you," it might be no trouble to write such a list. You've likely made such lists, or lists like them, at countless weekend workshops. What would be on it? Family, relationships, service, activism, creativity; you know that list by heart. But what does any of that mean when your troubles color everything?

Maybe the life purpose choice is to stop feeling so troubled. But how can that happen? Another trip to an outrageously expensive psychiatrist? Fifteen minutes of "And how are you sleeping?" and some next generation anti-depressant, which as you're quite aware guarantees you very little beyond some nasty side effects.

What then? A week-long workshop? Maybe an Andean shamanic journey or firewalking in the south of England? Well, there will likely be some congenial folks, some good massages, and some high points (and low points). But alleviation of the troubles? No. You know that firewalking, while hot and lovely, doesn't burn away the troubles.

You almost wish that you could become a nun, or a beachcomber, or a bomber pilot, or something! Something about that idea feels like the answer. But what sort of silly idea is "becoming somebody else"? Or...is that a silly idea? Maybe it's time to become, if not a bomber pilot, then a nun or a beachcomber?

Whatever the "answer" is, you know for certain that any life purpose choosing you do can't be done on a blank piece of paper, as if life were providing you with a neutral background against which to do that choosing. Blank sheets of paper are lovely for workshops! But in real life, the paper has caught on fire.

You know that any choosing you do must be accompanied by a fire extinguisher. Something is burning. Something inside of you is burning. What, become a bomber pilot? Well, no, that's silly! But something is burning, or demanding to be let out.

A lot of the time, you just want to cry. Tears and fire. Well, then, that is exactly the place from which your life purpose choosing must arise. Picture yourself as a bomber pilot. Picture yourself as a beachcomber. Picture yourself as a nun. What a trio! But that is a beginning.

The troubles are the challenge before you. Any menu of life purpose choices that you create must address them. Indeed, maybe this is a last chance, or who knows, a golden opportunity. Maybe this is a brand-new way to transform your misery. It must be worth trying.

CHAPTER 31

THREE LISTS

Let's paint a third picture of life purpose choosing. Let's imagine a woman we'll call Barbara, who was born Jewish and attended Hebrew school, then had some early flirtations with Eastern mysticism, vegetarianism, Buddhism, and Kabbalah, followed by a charismatic Catholic interlude (in part because of a boyfriend). Next came time in India and an ashram experience, followed by agnosticism, then atheism, and a period devoted to the Paleolithic diet. Currently, she is back to practicing Christianity.

Barbara has now come to a certain place in her life. Her husband of twenty-two years has walked out on her. Worse, he is majorly involved in the church the two of them have been attending, making continuing to attend that church awkward and unpleasant feeling. Worse still, he is bringing his new girlfriend with him to services.

What Barbara wants is revenge, not some life purpose choosing! In truth, she's angry and bitter. But her desire to choose "being love" and "turning the other cheek," as well as her belief that "compassion is the way" and "everything happens for a reason," are making it nearly impossible for her to feel and recognize her genuine emotions.

The life purpose choices populating her first list do not feel at all real to her. On that list are "stay calm," "stay connected to friends," "keep my job secure," and "find a new church." They are all plausible enough—but somehow they do not truly feel real. What is real at this moment? Barbara takes a walk downtown, does a little window shopping, and ponders the question, "What are my life purposes *right now*? What are they *really*?"

She comes home and makes a second list. It is a very strange list. On it are: "Have three margaritas every afternoon" and "sleep with Jack at work," as well as "burn down the garage" and "fly off to the Caribbean" and "f*** everything!" She has to smile a little looking at what she's written, her first smile in a long time. This list is at least more real! It may not be very upstanding, ethical, or righteous, but it represents how she actually feels much better than her first attempt did.

Barbara looks at the two lists side by side. It isn't precisely that the first list represents what she thinks she should do and the second list represents her real feelings; it's more complicated than that. Somehow the two lists recapitulate her whole life, some tense battle between seeking and being, between belief and roaring in self-expression.

Barbara decides to give herself the following sleep thinking prompt: "Can these two lists somehow go together?" She anticipates a restless night of tossing and turning. Instead, she sleeps amazingly well and wakes up realizing that she has had an epiphany. Although it is hard to put into words, it is something like, "I have a new definition of what 'right' means. I can judge the items on both lists against this new sense of 'rightness.' That's what choosing is going to look like from here on in!"

Barbara creates a new "list three." She realizes that her job is important to her—more important than ever. That goes on list three, along with "friendships" and "calmness." Finding a new church doesn't make it onto this new list, but "fly off to the Caribbean" does. Three margaritas a day has morphed to "buy a bottle of good champagne." With a bit of regret, she crosses off "burn down the garage" and "sleep with Jack at work." And she finds herself smiling just a little.

She has a new sense of what living means. There is to be no more seeking, and she has decided that ending all that seeking isn't going to feel like shutting down into icy coldness. This new way has warmth to it, liveliness, and a bit of pizzazz, as well as solidity balanced with an ever-changing sense of priorities. Barbara has plenty to put in her rearview mirror—but also an open road ahead of her.

The above scenario highlights something important about making your life purpose choices. Your first list may come from one place inside you, let's say from your good girl or good boy aspect. Your second list may come from a very different place—perhaps from your bad girl or bad boy aspect. (You may uncover other contrasting aspects within yourself, such as practical vs. romantic.) So, a third list may well be needed, a synthesis that better represents just who you would like to be and what you would like to do at this precise moment in time.

CHAPTER 32

HUDDLED IN A BUNKER

Let's imagine that you've been conscripted to fight in a war where your country is the unjust aggressor. The leader of your country is a dictator, half the population has turned to fascism, and you have no idea who to trust—including which members of your own family. Isn't it absurd to talk about life purpose choosing as you huddle in a bunker in some foreign land, waiting to attack or be attacked?

Your life was a very different thing only months ago. You were a student studying literature, you went to parties, you argued loudly about whether this book or that book was really a classic of world literature. Six months later, you found yourself on a rifle range, learning to shoot, with the officer in charge yelling at you incessantly. Some days you cleaned your rifle, some days you peeled potatoes. Now you've been loaded on a truck headed to the front lines.

One choice is to desert. That is on your mind constantly. A second choice is to take as many drugs as your fellow soldiers are taking and stay high. A third choice is—strangely enough—to excel, to be a model soldier, maybe so as to fulfill your own ego needs and "feel like a man." A fourth choice is to put your head down, never volunteer, stay as far back as possible, and maybe survive.

This is nothing like deciding on health, creativity, service, relationships, and activism as life purpose choices! This is choosing under duress, with tremendously limited possibilities, all of them bad. Can deserting or staying high even be called choosing? But yes, those are choices; and this is the array of life purpose choices available to you in this situation. Like everyone, everywhere, you have been dealt a hand and must play it.

Let's say that you choose hunkering down and trying to survive. How do you manufacture any enthusiasm for such a choice? How can you be bright and cheery and oh-so-proud that you've made a clear choice? It's unlikely that you can. But even if you can't, that doesn't exempt you from making other choices, too.

You must decide how you'll relate to your fellow soldiers. Will you make friends or stay aloof? You must decide how you'll relate to orders. Will you follow those orders bound to get you killed, or will you reconsider whether to desert? You must decide if this is a moment for survival at all costs or whether you will set some limits on survival tactics. Will you steal that unguarded sleeping bag or freeze? These are your new choices.

Ah, you may say, I'm not facing anything like that. But millions of people are, and you may, too. World-shifting scenarios happen, and many of them do not allow for brilliant choices. I remember a moment during my Army days in Korea where I stupidly left my sleeping bag back at base camp and almost shot the soldier next to me for his sleeping bag. Fortunately for both of us, I didn't. But that is what life can throw at us.

Millions of people become refugees. Millions of people face life-altering medical diagnoses. Millions of people fall under fascist rule. Millions of people fall prey to a collapsed economy. Millions of people are starving. And to all of them I say, no hardship turns the process of life purpose decisions into something ridiculous. If anything, it makes it all the more important. That is our poignant reality.

I could present many more scenarios for us to consider and learn from— as many as there are people. But these four may prove enough to give you the flavor of the enterprise I'm inviting you to embrace. It is not "make a nice list of life purpose choices, rank them in order, and live happily ever after." Rather, it's the following: choosing your life purposes is a better bet than not choosing them.

The choices available to you may be limited or even terrible, but where does not choosing among them leave you? Failing to decide puts you back in a place of weakly waiting for answers, as if you were waiting for the phone to ring. There is no one on the other end of that phone, and there is no phone, either. It is on your shoulders to choose, even if your shoulders are slumped.

CHAPTER 33

BRICK WALLS AND ROLLERCOASTERS

Did those scenarios alert you to the way that life purpose choosing happens in the context of a real life lived? Real life is messy; real life is tangled. In real life, we have multiple motivations, radical changes of plans, and seismic shifts in what we feel and believe and what we think possible. This is choosing while on a rollercoaster, with brick walls at every turn. Who asked for that?

Imagine that you're a painter and you learn that you are HIV-positive. Before your diagnosis, you painted urban landscapes. After that diagnosis, you start painting blood drops as seen under a microscope. Your world, your life, and your subject matter have shifted. But painting is still important to you. Is such a radical shift in subject matter the same as a change in life purpose choice? What would you say?

Let's say that intimacy is important to you. Your husband of fifty years passes away. You still crave intimacy, but you can't see yourself dating. Intimacy still matters to you, but the path to it is blocked by grief and by your skepticism about dating at your age. Since it is blocked, intimacy appears not to be a life purpose choice at this moment—or maybe even any longer. Or is it still? Yes? No?

Imagine that you want to be a chemist, but you hate graduate school. You've fallen behind, and you doubt that you can master the material you'll have to know. Chemistry is becoming less and less important to you—in fact, you've started to hate it. But is it chemistry that is less important to you, or just that mastering it is hard? Given everything, what sense can you make of life purpose choosing? Can you continue to choose chemistry while failing at it?

What if you've always held that family is important to you? Let's say it is a no-brainer life purpose choice of yours. But no one in your family seems to want to get together anymore. There is a strange coldness among the children, as if each is holding a grudge. All plans to gather fall apart for one reason or another. Family remains a life purpose choice of yours—but what does that mean if no one is talking to one another?

In another scenario, imagine that you're clever and have always been quick. But you never wanted to be a fast-talking lawyer, a ready-with-an-answer accountant, or a brilliant academic. Strange to say, you've never been able to find a setting to match for your wit or a context that whets your appetite. You've come to identify with Kafka's Hunger Artist, for whom no food appealed. What will the enterprise of life purpose choosing look like for you, given your lack of appetite?

What you know how to do is no longer wanted. You've been replaced by automation, by cheaper labor, by changing tastes, by technology, by AI. You and everyone in your industry know that you "must do something else." Of course! But you've been doing what you've been doing for thirty years. It's your identity, your skill set, your everything. How dare someone tell you that you should snap your fingers and "make some new choices"? How dare they?

You're a dancer in your mid-thirties, at the end of your dance career. The cliché next thing to do is to open a small dance studio. You can't tolerate that thought. You love dance, but picturing that dance studio brings you to tears. It reeks of failure. And you don't want to teach dance—you want to dance. You want to be seen. You want to move audiences. But that's just about all behind you now. Good choices? Ha!

This may have you thinking that the notion of life purpose choosing is daft. But it isn't daft. Rather, it's our very best way of dealing with life. It is life that is daft. What life throws at us, it will throw at us whether or not we adopt this philosophy of making our life purpose choices and then doing our best to live them.

The rollercoaster rides and brick walls of life are coming either way, whether we live intentionally or live pointlessly. We therefore respond intentionally, because that is the better idea. We make a decision about whether we hate chemistry or if we perhaps just need a tutor. We endeavor to do the next right, wise thing while burdened with a new HIV-positive diagnosis or grieving the death of a spouse. We do not say, "The hell with life!" We buy our ticket and get back on the rollercoaster.

CHAPTER 34

FIRST CHOOSING

Choosing your life purposes means identifying what's important to you and then organizing your life around those choices. It may be important to you that you take a walk every day for fifteen minutes, that you find a new job or a new career, that you improve your relationship with your son or daughter, or that you worry less. It could be anything— anything that's important to you.

But is taking a walk for fifteen minutes every day "as important" as finding a new career? Can deciding to confront your alcohol consumption go on the same list as deciding to write a novel or deciding to advance at work? How can we balance purposes involving our inner life with the outer world? How can such different things—some that seem small and some that seem gigantic—be considered together? Isn't that just too messy and confusing?

It can be messy and confusing. But it can also be simple. Just open your mind and your heart to the question, "What's important to me?" and let whatever wants to percolate up have its own equal place on your list. Even if your list looks as strange and disjointed as "feel less lonely, be more creative, lose thirty pounds, figure out why my teenage daughter is so unhappy, find my spiritual core, and get the spare room straightened up," that is a perfect beginning!

Try not to censor yourself. Let everything that wants to bubble up in response to the question "What's important to me?" have a place on your list. What if your list grows to seventy things? That's okay! There's an organizational step coming where you'll do some sorting and get to put those disjointed things into their bushel baskets. For now, just be open to what wants to bubble up. Let your list be as long as it wants to be and as weird as it wants to be!

Once you've created that list, take a breath, maybe take a stroll, and then come back to the task of organizing your list. See if the items on your list can be combined together by placing them in one or another of the following twenty categories: physical health, emotional well-being, work and career, parenting and family, intimate relationships, friendships, calmness and stress reduction, creativity, service, activism, mood elevation, hobbies and relaxation, finances, life organization, time management, lifelong learning, growth and healing, adventure, spirituality and mystery, and life philosophy.

For instance, "exercise once a day," "lose thirty pounds," "get an annual check-up," "find some sunlight during this dark winter," "stop sitting on the couch so much," and "get to bed a little earlier" might all go under "health." Having done that sorting and placed them there, you would now be able to say, "My health is one of my life purpose choices."

Perhaps at the end of this process you'll end up with between three and five clear life purpose choices; for example, physical health, relationships, career, creativity, and emotional well-being. But what about the leftover bits that haven't quite fit into any category? Simply add them to your list of current life purposes, since they do in fact matter to you right now. It's doesn't matter if that makes your list look odd!

For instance, maybe "get the spare room straightened up" connects to creativity, because you want that room as a painting studio. But maybe it doesn't connect to anything—you're just tired of it being a mess. So, you would just add it to your list, and your list in the above example would then read physical health, relationships, career, creativity, emotional well-being, and getting the spare room straightened up. Yes, that sounds a bit odd. But that's your reality!

Work on your list until you feel pretty settled on your life purpose choices. If possible, try to keep your list manageable, since it's rather daunting to try to deal with too many life purpose choices at one time. Maybe some of them, some of the "sort of important but not that important" ones, can be tabled for the moment. If possible, it would be good to keep your list to half a dozen choices or fewer. But it's *your* list!

If I were aiming you in a linear way, your next tasks would be to identify what kind of actions go with each of your life purpose choices and then add those actions to your daily and weekly calendars. But before we go there, I'd like to present you with a picture of many "classic" life purpose choices—that is, things that human beings typically find important. I want to do this to enrich your thinking on what constitutes a life purpose choice and to make sure that you haven't missed any choices that may in fact be genuinely important to you.

CHAPTER 35

CLASSIC LIFE PURPOSE CHOICES

Over the next several chapters, I'll present some classic life purpose choices; that is, things that lots of people find important and choices that many people make. Some are so well-known and obvious that I'll spend only a few sentences on them. Others that are less well-known will get more attention. At the end of this mini-examination, I'll give you the chance to revisit your choices and see if you want to shift and expand them in the light of this discussion.

Love and Intimacy. We are built to experience love as meaningful and important. Unless life has harmed us to such an extent that we have stopped daring to love, or unless we've become so self-involved that all the love we need is self-love, love is a likely life purpose choice for us. You could love today—all it takes is a softening of your heart and an object of affection. Think of the words in the family of love, words like affection, kindness, generosity, and intimacy. They paint a rich picture of what loving means. Wouldn't you like to make love a life purpose choice?

Friendships and Peer Relationships. This life purpose is about creating friendships with others, making connections in your field of work, business, and career, and in its essence, being human in the presence of other human beings. Protecting our individuality requires that we remain fundamentally separate—but while separateness has its place, friendships and peer relationships are classic life purpose choices.

Parenting and Family. Our mate and our children are important to us—that goes without saying. But life has a way of distancing us from our family members as we and they go about the business of living. Classic life purpose choices that relate to connecting with family include: remembering that they are important; paying more attention to them; making more time for them; and helping them where they need help and asking for their help when we need help.

Work and Career. "Career" is the word we use for our desire to work in a productive, effective way in a field of work we have chosen. It isn't synonymous with "making a living." A career poet, for example, has little chance of living on the money she makes from her poetry. But she can still have a real career, with the psychological rewards, real-world successes, and experiences of meaning that come with a career. Many people consider their career important, invest their time, money, and human capital in their work, and opt to make career a prime life purpose choice.

Health and Well-Being. Our physical health and our emotional well-being are obvious life purpose choices. These two broad categories might include sub-choices like dieting, getting more exercise, elevating our mood, finding a better work-life balance, reducing stress and managing anxiety, ending a toxic relationship, attending to a chronic illness, and so on. It's entirely likely that these two will find their way onto your list of life purpose choices.

Creativity and Self-Expression. Creativity is a large, rich word that stands for the way we make use of our inner resources and our talents. We can approach anything creatively—creativity is not reserved for certain pursuits like writing a novel or inventing software. You could choose to approach some challenge at work with grudging energy and a feeling of boredom, or you can decide to invest something of yourself in it by engaging your imagination and approaching it creatively. For many people, creativity is among their top life purpose choices.

Growth and Healing. This category covers all sorts of life purpose choices we might make: recovering from an addiction, healing from early childhood trauma, upgrading our personality and becoming more the person we would like to be, gaining personal insights and learning from our experiences, and so on. For many people, this is their number one life purpose choice because they know that nothing else in life will work particularly well if they don't pay attention to necessary processes like healing from trauma or entering recovery. **Spirituality and Mystery.** Countless people consider spirituality important to them, however they define that elusive something. For one person, gaining insight using divination methods such as tarot cards and astrology will be important; for another, it will be their traditional religious faith. For others, it could be a philosophical tradition like stoicism. Indeed, many people organize their whole life around a spiritual or existential belief system, and for them, nothing is more important.

All of these possibilities are classic life purpose choices. Many of them may already have made their way onto your list. Now that you've been reminded of them, you may see others you want to add to your life purpose list. Let your list grow as long as you like! It can be pruned, prioritized, and organized later. For now, allow it to expand to include whatever you deem important.

CHAPTER 36

CLASSIC CHOICES: EXCELLENCE AND ACHIEVEMENT

We are built with an ego and the powerful desires that come with it; many of us also experience the drive to excel and achieve. Even if we have decided to live in a detached, phlegmatic, and philosophical way—which might serve us beautifully—we may still cherish achievement and excellence as life purpose choices.

A cloistered monk may still want the wine he produces to be excellent and perhaps even to win awards. Such desires amount to life purpose choices for him, even if he views his own attachment to excellence and accolades with some irony. Yes, we may view achievement and excellence a little wryly, yet at the same time consider them seriously important. No paradox or conflict there!

It may strike us as important to make a name for ourselves in our field, to complete large-scale projects, or to get really good at something. Maybe excelling at something has provided us with experiences of meaning in the past or has even been a source of long-lasting meaning. It's no wonder that we might consider excellence and achievement as life purposes!

There is nothing paradoxical about having "just being" and contentment as life purpose choices while at the same time including excellence and achievement as life purposes as well. You might sit contently by a pond for an hour, soaking up the sun, living that life purpose. Then, an hour later, having returned to your work, you might achieve a breakthrough and jump up and down. Both experiences matter!

Sad to say, we may lose our taste for excellence and achievement over time. As children, we start out with two enthusiasms, both of which appeal to us: we love to experiment, and we love to excel. Soon, though, because we're pressured to get things right, we start to lose our taste for experimentation; and because much of what we do doesn't rise to the level of excellence, we begin to fear that excellence isn't in us.

Out of this dynamic a middle-of-the-road approach to life often arises, one where we neither experiment nor try to excel. So many people live this way! They have given up on achievement and excellence and do "just enough," or barely that. And, of course, they are down on themselves because they know that they are not living up to their own potential.

This is your opportunity to revisit these potential life purpose choices. If you want to, you could decide to bite into something rich, important, and difficult, and do it really well. You can decide to do this even if years have gone by and you're wondering if it's too late. Maybe you'll flounder at first; maybe you'll make some heroic messes. But excellence might be the end result. And if it is, wouldn't that feel excellent?

I've worked with many coaching clients who've been bolstered by some particular achievement in their lives—something that now works for them as a sort of reservoir of meaning, a place they can tap into when they need a meaning boost. Maybe it was finally getting their novel published, or a song they wrote being covered by a well-known recording artist. Perhaps it was the staged reading of their play, or a themed exhibition of their photographs showing in a high-end gallery.

They accomplished something—and the memory lingers. Consider that possibility. You might experience meaning while you are doing some excellent work. That would be lovely. But you might also experience that certain feeling months, years, or even decades after the fact, when, sitting by the fire and recollecting, you remember your achievement and feel pride and a sense of accomplishment. Isn't that the beauty in life?

Excellence and achievement are among the gifts that keep on giving. They reward you long after the work is done. As you work to identify what's important to you at this point in your life, consider the possibility that these two classic life purpose choices might want to make it onto your list. Give them a chance, even if thinking about them generates a few watts of anxiety.

CHAPTER 37

CLASSIC CHOICES: EXPERIMENTATION

It may not have occurred to you to consider "experimentation" as a life purpose choice. But if you are interested in personal growth, self-actualization, creativity, healing, recovery, or some other life purpose choice that requires genuine learning and self-knowledge, then you want to add "experimentation" to your menu of life purpose choices, because trial-and-error experimentation is the best way to learn anything.

Consider two scenarios. In the first, you paint the sort of painting you know how to paint. Maybe you end up with a result that you like as well as one that your collectors like. But won't you feel just a little hollow, dissatisfied, and even down? Quite likely. Even if we do excellent work, we can still bore ourselves and feel as if we are not manifesting our true potential if we simply repeat ourselves.

Say on the other hand that you devote every Saturday to some wild painting experiments; even if they don't pan out and even if they cost you some expensive paint and canvas, aren't you likely to break free of your usual constraints, imagery, and way of doing things? If you've been craving that feeling of meaning, and maybe wondering why it feels so elusive given that you've been painting well and selling well, isn't it possible running an experiment of this sort could be just the ticket?

Experimenting is a crucial feature of creativity, growth, and learning. We can't learn a new art medium unless we experiment with it. We can't learn how to run our business except through trial-and-error experimentation. We can't pursue a line of research unless we are willing to entertain an idea, turn it over, and see if it works—that is, unless we are willing to experiment with ideas.

We can't know whether it's better to travel down this path or that path unless we experiment with one path or the other. Yes, maybe we should try to look into our crystal ball and see the future so as to avoid dead ends and pratfalls that we could see coming if we anticipated them. But at the same time, looking into that crystal ball isn't the same as living. Ultimately, we must run life experiments: when we marry, when we have children, when we choose a career, when we drop this and pick up that.

If you've lost your taste for experimentation, you might want to see if you can reacquire it by choosing experimentation as one of your life purpose choices. Pick a beautiful experiment—a small one or a large one, one near to your heart, one that piques your curiosity, or one that you think might serve your ends—and leap in. Remember that it's an experiment! As much as you may have a hunch about the outcome, you can't really know the results beforehand. That's why it's called an experiment!

The special quality of a genuine experiment is that you really don't know what the outcome will be. Many experiments in the sciences and the social sciences aren't genuine experiments, because the researchers need a certain outcome—to justify their funding, for prestige reasons, and so on—and whether consciously or unconsciously, they manipulate the experiment so as to get the outcome they want. How meaningful is such pseudo-experimenting going to feel?

Here's how a genuine experiment looks. A singer/songwriter client of mine wondered if he could write a musical. He could have just wondered—but instead, he went ahead with an experiment of turning his ideas into songs and a script. Creating that first song felt wonderfully meaningful. Its existence then prompted the next experiment, to see if the second song he had in mind worked with the first one. That second experiment injected another dose of meaning into his life, motivating him to continue creating.

Soon—really amazingly quickly—he had the full score and script done. Within months he got a grant to hire singers and actors to put together a staged reading of his musical. Could there be any doubt that entering that room for the first time, that room full of eager actor/singers and musicians, was one of the highlights of his life? Doesn't it go without saying that experimenting to see if he could create a musical paid off handsomely?

Even if the experiment you run doesn't end in the result you want—my client's musical still hasn't made its way to Broadway—running this experiment enriched his life. If you can let go of needing a successful outcome and if you can rejoice in the process and the experience, you may discover that adding "experimentation" to your menu of life purpose choices enriches your life. Put on your thinking cap and ask yourself, "What juicy experiment might I run?" Surprise yourself!

CHAPTER 38

CLASSIC CHOICES: SELF-ACTUALIZATION

Self-actualization is a lovely word that stands for our desire to make the most of our talents, insights, interests, and inner resources. Instead of using only a small portion of our total being, just enough to get by, we make the conscious, ultimately heroic decision to employ our full intelligence, our emotional capital, and our best personality qualities in the service of something: a cause, a problem, an artistic creation, a way of being.

Of course, this is hard. It isn't so easy to lead with our best personality—we're rather shadowy, defensive creatures who find countless ways not to manifest courage, discipline, fortitude, and those other qualities that represent us at our best. Likewise, the process is complicated and arduous: we might want to use our full potential in the service of writing our novel, say, but that embroils us in the very real process of novel-writing, with all of its mysteries and difficulties.

Despite these difficulties, we know in our heart of hearts that we would love to fully utilize our potential and make ourselves proud by doing so. Self-actualization is how you become your best self—moment by moment making the conscious decision to tap into your potentiality and harness your power. When you do so—when you exhaust yourself in the service of something you deem important—there is every chance that the feeling of meaning will attach to your efforts.

A client we'll call Harry came to see me, complaining that he felt as if he was leading what he called a shadow life. He explained that he wasn't talking about depression or despair or even a pervasive sense of the blues, but something else, something that was hard to name but he was feeling all the time, but especially when he awoke and when he went to bed. "At those times," he said, "I just feel so small, like I'm three inches tall."

"What's your hunch about it?" I wondered. "What do you think is going on?" He shook his head. "I have no idea," he said. "At work, at the big law office where I work, I'm given all the toughest cases, because I'm smart and reliable and resourceful. So, it's not like I don't have the opportunity to dive into things and do real work. And yet..."

"It sounds like you're using a lot of yourself already," I replied. "But if the cases mattered to you more or differently, is there even more of you that you would use?" "Absolutely!" he exclaimed. "What would the difference be?" I wondered. "Not the number of hours you put in—you already put in a ton of hours, I'm guessing. Not the attention you pay—you already pay full attention. What would be different?"

He thought about that. Finally, he shook his head. "I can't find the way to say it. It's as if, with my current cases, I'm sitting down, and if the work mattered to me, I would suddenly stand up." "And when you're sitting down?" I wondered. "I'm three inches tall." We both nodded. "So," I continued, "the conclusion is?" "I don't know. What is the conclusion?" Harry replied.

"Well, I can't quit my job." Harry said after a moment. "That would be scary and irresponsible. Plus, I would just have to find a new one, and that one would likely be worse, not better, and there I would be again." Now ought to come the happy ending...if there had been a happy ending. But, like millions of our fellow human beings, Harry, in his exact set of circumstances, had no easy answer available.

"But I can try one thing," he said suddenly. "I can at least try to identify what sort of cause would really move me. I can't take on cases there, wherever 'there' is, because I'm just too busy. But maybe I could at least come to know where 'there' is." "That is one brilliant gambit!" I replied. "You know what?" Harry continued. "I feel one inch taller already!" And we had our first good laugh.

It's unlikely that we can simply snap our fingers and self-actualize. Too much reality stands in the way. But we can treat self-actualization as a prime life purpose choice and a high-bar goal—and as something that is possible. Even just having that conversation with ourselves about what manifesting and actualizing our potential could look like might start the ball rolling!

CHAPTER 39

CLASSIC CHOICES: PLEASURE AND CONTENTMENT

In a well-rounded life where we are endeavoring to live our life purposes, pleasure ought to have its rightful place. Yes, if our life was only about garnering pleasure, we might rightly feel that we had strayed too far from our values and our principles by living just for enjoyment. But if we're crafting a value-based life and living in all sorts of responsible ways, then certainly we're entitled to include pleasure!

Take pleasure in the grandeur of the night sky—just so long as you keep your feet on the ground. Take pleasure in what cadmium red makes you feel when you see it—just so long as you don't begin to spend more time with color than with your children. Take pleasure in an orgasm—just so long as it isn't at the expense of betraying someone. Mind your ethics—and enjoy life, too! Pleasure is legitimate.

It may seem surprising that I'm stopping to remind you that pleasure is an important and legitimate life purpose choice. But that reminder is necessary. People not only forget that pleasure is important and that it is available to them—they often actively ward off the experience of pleasure. So many people are doing that!

For a variety of reasons, among them cultural and religious injunctions against experiencing pleasure, a superstitious reluctance to admit that we actually enjoy pleasure, and the idea that pleasure is too low a thing to honor, people regularly refuse to view pleasure as a legitimate life purpose choice. Are you in that boat?

Why not take pleasure in all the usual places—in that piece of apple pie, that orgasm, that massage, that comfy bed, that morning cup of coffee? And why not add new and different pleasures? Pleasure is not a suspect or second-rate life purpose choice, not in a life made rich and rounded by a variety of value-based efforts. Life need not to be experienced as a dry sort of thing. Joy, pleasure, contentment...have them!

Contentment and pleasure are cousins. You might well want to cultivate the mindset and habit of contentment. Of course, you could rehash your dark past, and by doing so, make sure that the present and the future resemble it. Or you can opt to enjoy what can be enjoyed, to take pleasure, to angle for contentment, to relax—to be that sort of person.

Yes, there are always ethical considerations. A hot shower may give you pleasure—but how long a shower should you take in the middle of a drought? Eating a bagel with cream cheese and lox may give you pleasure—but what if your health demands that you avoid cream cheese? As with all of our life purposes, there are always considerations. Pleasure may be pure, so to speak, but there is always a context.

So, maybe you can't have that cream cheese. But you can still have it in memory. Experiences like pleasure and states like contentment exist in memory and can be conjured up right now, today. Was it one of your great pleasures to swim in the lake as a child? Retrieve that memory. Did you find contentment on that walk through the forest? Remember it. Conjuring such memories are choices you make, choices on the side of contentment and pleasure.

And don't forget relaxation. We know that stress harms and even kills, yet we still have trouble giving relaxation its due and holding it as part of the life purpose choice of paying attention to our health. Diet, yes. Exercise, yes. But sitting with the sun shining down on you and doing nothing at all for ten minutes straight? How improper that can feel! Shouldn't you be doing the laundry instead? How dare you just sit there!

Pleasure. Contentment. Joy. Relaxation. Aren't these worthy? Aren't they legitimate? I invite you to consider if, maybe inadvertently and accidentally, you've excluded these from your life. They warm life, they elevate your mood, they provide you with memories, and they flat-out feel good. Yes, of course, we intend to do right. But can't we also feel good?

CHAPTER 40

CLASSIC CHOICES: SERVICE AND STEWARDSHIP

Being of service is a classic life purpose choice. Even if we have powerful ego needs and a bit of everyday grandiosity and narcissism built into us, we may still choose to be of service, to accomplish good works, and to be a good steward.

Pointing someone in the right direction, providing a useful service, or easing someone's distress are acts that match our values and meet our desire to connect with our fellow human beings. One heaping plate of service after another might not amount to a balanced life purposes meal. But as one among our several life purpose choices, service might serve us beautifully.

Formal volunteering is just one sort of service. It is also a great service, for example, to make things easier rather than harder for the people around you, to hold the vision and values of your community, company, or family when that vision blurs and those values stray, to stretch out your hand to a neighbor, or to spontaneously provide your expertise when your skills are needed.

Another face of service is stewardship. Nature has provided us with a sense of right and wrong and an understanding of ideas like responsibility, mutuality, and shared humanity. As a result, many people want to help save the world or at least their corner of the world, perhaps by becoming an environmental activist. That's stewardship.

We can aim to steward our children, civil rights, democratic institutions, the environment, or anything small or large that we think is worth our concern. It could be the oceans; it could be the stream at the edge of town. It could be freedom of speech; it could be the freedom of one person to speak. Maybe you'd like to pick something to steward—a person, an ideal, a resource—as one of your life purpose choices?

Service and stewardship are good works: real work of our own choosing that reflects our principles and our values. Maybe your everyday job feels short on real value, but you need to stay the course because that work pays the bills; in that case, perhaps you would like to supplement that work-for-pay with good works of your own choosing?

Of course, your results may fall far short of your hopes and expectations. You may intellectually understand why you are doing what you have chosen to do, because it matches your values, principles, and life purposes, but nevertheless you may still dislike and resent what you are doing, perhaps because the nonprofit where you volunteer is unpleasantly political and/or because so little changes out in the world. That happens!

The greater the investment of your time and energy, the larger the potential crisis. It is good if we can handle it when something we thought amounted to a solid life purpose choice falls short in the living. This doesn't mean you are unable to effectively serve or be a good steward, or that you cannot engage in good works. The more accurate conclusion to reach is that life is a complicated, paradoxical, and very mixed affair; that's just how life is.

Living ethically in the real world of contradictions, complications, and competing values is no easy matter. But we know why we do it: we may be doing a little good. Taking action of this sort makes us feel more alive.

Your life will likely feel more meaningful if you remember to include service, stewardship, and other good works among your life purpose choices. Right now, you may feel reluctant to look in those directions. It's possible you feel that you don't have the time, or perhaps you doubt that you will get enough of a payoff, since it can be tough to make enough to live on in a life devoted to service. Maybe you are down on people and aren't feeling much like helping them at present. Understood. But think about it. Maybe service and stewardship ought to go on your list.

CHAPTER 41

CLASSIC CHOICES: ACTIVISM AND REBELLION

Activism is defined as "vigorous campaigning to bring about political or social change." Some people live an activist life and number activism and rebellion among their prime life purpose choices. Considerably more people are occasional activists, moved to stand up in reaction to something that has happened, like a pressing threat to a civil right or a political right. Even though their activism is only occasional, it appears on their list of life purpose choices.

Do activism and rebellion appear on your list? Maybe they have not occurred to you much as life purposes; or maybe they are on your mind much of the time, but you just can't find a good reason to bother, given how little power and influence you possess. It can seem completely absurd to imagine standing up to billion-dollar influencers, fascist dictators, entrenched institutions, and the powers that be. Raise a lone fist? How absurd!

Of course, it can seem absurd to bother. How can one lone individual do much of anything? Will anyone take notice if a protest march has ten thousand people in it, or ten thousand and one? But we understand that such absurdity must not be allowed to stand as an excuse for inaction. We nod at that absurdity, we give it its due, and then we act: you acknowledge the absurdity without letting it defeat you!

In Albert Camus's famous fable "The Myth of Sisyphus," Sisyphus, who has been condemned by the gods to roll a rock up a mountain every single day for all eternity, smiles at the absurdity of his situation. But in his peculiar way, he has it easy. Rendered completely impotent by the gods, he can smile the dignified, mostly vacant smile of a man who is no longer with us, a living dead man, one who is smiling from the afterlife.

Sisyphus can take no action in the real world. He can respond with dignity and his peculiar smile to his situation; but his situation is not yours. He is trapped in an even more monumental sense than you are. You can still do some good! You are not Sisyphus. Your delicate amount of freedom, while pitted against an ocean of absurdity, is indeed your burden to bear; but it is also your responsibility to make use of that freedom.

So, you acknowledge that it is absurd to stand up while tired, out of sorts, unequal to the occasion, and only wanting brunch. That absurdity be damned, you act. You rise to your feet and stand. Sisyphus may be wearing his patented ironic smile. Your smile is graver. You have your small portion of freedom, that portion that you are obliged to use. Maybe you find that you can't smile at all. But you act nonetheless.

We really do not like the idea of giving in and giving up. In Kafka's novel *The Trial*, the protagonist, Josef K., hunts for rational answers to his absurd situation, which finds him sentenced to death for no reason that he can fathom. Finally, he is absurdly executed. Watching him, we want to scream, "Stop it already, K.! Don't you see that rebellion is the only answer!" We want K. to refuse to sheepishly play along; we want him to denounce the injustice of his punishment. Please, K., rebel!

Well, but what can rebellion look like to, say, an old woman in a wheelchair parked in a nursing home corridor? Or to a refugee carrying his belongings on his back? Or to a gay teenager trapped in a claustrophobic town? What then? What can rebellion look like to each of them? For the old woman, it might mean taking three painful steps with her walker. The refugee might become a refugee camp leader. The gay youth might plot his escape. These are the things they might try.

Each can do something, and each must do something. There is no overarching principle we can offer, except the principle of radical self-authorship. A human being can stand up, even if he or she can't literally stand up. No one is in a perfect position to rebel. We are all too burdened, too constrained, too conflicted, too human. So, instead, we awkwardly stand on one foot and rebel while tilting.

Like so many of the life purpose choices we've been discussing, activism and rebellion are unlikely to find their way to the top of your list of life purpose choices, except maybe now and then, in reaction to some threat or happenstance. But they can hold an honorable place on your list, not at the top but also not at the bottom. As we approach your second round of choosing, give this some thought.

CHAPTER 42

CLASSIC CHOICES: APPRECIATION AND GRATITUDE

Many people live a gloomy, pessimistic, critical and self-critical life. They may have abundant reasons for living this way, ranging from a cultural imperative to not take pleasure from life to a harsh upbringing that has made them sadder and smaller than they otherwise might have been.

These reasons are powerful and pertinent—but they do not amount to a life sentence. Even people who have been harmed in these ways still have as one of their life purpose choices the possibility of appreciating life and expressing their gratitude where gratitude is due.

Life feels more meaningful when you appreciate what can be appreciated: a juicy apple, a day of rest, an accomplishment, a child at play, a summer breeze. If each of these experiences is dismissed the instant it is experienced—if the instant you see a child smile, you say to yourself, "Just wait until she has to find a job!"—then you are robbing yourself, existentially speaking. You may well be right that she has a hard life ahead of her, but thinking that thought when you see her smile robs your own life of joy, meaning, and motivation.

I began coaching a lawyer who had left the corporate world to become a high-paid consultant. He had a lot: money, prestige, a big home, a healthy, loving family, friends, and more. But he was pestered by three thoughts: "I'm not doing enough," "I could be of some real service," and "life isn't feeling all that meaningful." Those three thoughts plagued him.

"So," I asked him, "Shall we get you some experiences of meaning right now?" He shook his head. "That is such a weird way to think of it! Can you please explain what you mean?" I did. I explained that meaning was merely a feeling, and that, by contrast, life purpose was a choice. I explained the difference between "the purpose of life" and identifying and living one's life purpose choices. I gave him my pitch.

"I think I get it," he said. "So...I could have more of those experiences right now?"

"With luck. That's why I call trying out things 'meaning opportunities,' because they may potentially produce that feeling, but there are no guarantees that they will. They are things to try—and then you get to see if they come with the feeling of meaning or not."

"Well, okay, what should I try?" he wondered.

I thought about that. "I could make many sorts of recommendations. And we could chat about those many recommendations. But I want to float one in particular—appreciation. You have a lot to appreciate in your life. But you are dashing forward, pestering yourself with 'next,' and 'more,' and this and that. Tell me: do you appreciate what you have?"

He hesitated. "No, I don't think I do." We made a plan. That night, he would appreciate his dinner. He would appreciate his wife. He would appreciate his son. He would appreciate his daughter. He would appreciate the basketball game he intended to watch and appreciate that he could watch it, that technology brought his favorite team into his living room. He would appreciate his garden, his study with its view of the mountains, the fact that his parents were still healthy...the list was long.

The following Monday, he reported via email that, despite the weirdness of the enterprise, he was feeling a great deal better. By virtue of him appreciating it, life had become "more meaningful" immediately. He had to laugh. He signed off with, "That was all there was to it?" Well, no, not quite. But while those hungers and cravings were bound to continue, he at least now had some mechanisms to better live his life purposes: gratitude and appreciation.

And if a person doesn't have all that this lucky lawyer possessed? Well, an unlucky person can still find aspects of life to appreciate. If he is down on his luck, down on life, and upset about life's inequities and tribulations, it will be much harder for him to appreciate his existence—and, indeed, he may not choose appreciation as one of his life purpose choices. Maybe he'll find rebellious activism or creative effort more appropriate. But I would still invite him to consider: even in his less-than-perfect circumstances, might gratitude and appreciation serve him?

CHAPTER 43

CLASSIC CHOICES: WAYS OF BEING

A life purpose choice need not only be about "doing something," as in writing a novel, serving in a soup kitchen, or walking ten thousand steps a day. It can also be about "being a certain way," for instance being calmer or more passionate. Other "ways of being" choices include being more peaceful, more optimistic, more adventurous, more thoughtful, more engaged, more spontaneous, or more self-confident.

Take self-confidence. What might it look like to choose self-confidence as a life purpose choice? The following are examples of concrete actions that might support such a choice. Once a day, or more often than that, you might visualize successfully completing a long-term goal while saying the words, "I feel confident." Or you might pencil on your weekly calendar a "calculated risk" that you intend to take at work—for example, asking for a raise. Or—what might you try?

Maybe you'd like to be calmer and make calmness a life purpose choice. How might you do that? By affirming, "I am calm"? By creating a "ceremony of calmness"? By refusing to create unnecessary dramas? By meditating? By penciling relaxation onto your daily to-do list? By doing things that calm you, like listening to music or hiking in nature? Or just by being calmer?

Being a certain way may involve "doing," like taking a risk if you're practicing self-confidence, or meditating if you're seeking calmness. But it might also amount more to an attitude change or a personality upgrade than any particular action or set of actions. You might become a calmer person, a more passionate person, a more optimistic person. You would then just be that person. Voila!

Consider the choice of being "adventurous." You could go on actual safaris or really go out and skydive. But you could also react internally in new ways, for example, by letting yourself light up inside when you think about going on an adventure, rather than feeling scared and shutting down. You might nod internally at the thought of a grand vision quest or a quixotic undertaking, rather than shaking your head in an internal refusal. No one would see you being more adventurous—but inside, you would be.

So, a life purpose choice of this sort might not come with any overt actions. There might not be anything to pencil into your schedule or add to your to-do list. There would instead be a new you to manifest, a new you who is more passionate, more self-confident, calmer, or whatever you choose. We might only see you smile rather than frown or leap in rather than retreat. That smile and that leap might not have appeared on your to-do list, but aren't they of the highest importance?

Take "engaged" as the way that you want to be and as a new life purpose choice. You have all of these other life purpose choices to manifest—career, family, creativity, and all the others. But now, you are viewing them through the lens of engagement. You aren't writing your novel dispassionately—you're engaged. You aren't half-listening to the story about school that your seven-year-old is trying to tell you—you're engaged. By making engagement a life purpose choice, you enrich all of your other life purpose choices.

By "being" differently, we can improve everything. We might even free ourselves from what may seem like a permanent, baked-in ailment, some long-term sadness, anxiety, or distractibility. Who knows how deeply baked in such phenomena are? Maybe new optimism might lessen your sadness or new calmness might reduce your distractibility. Isn't that worth considering and trying out?

Another way of saying this is that you might want to choose upgrading your personality as a life purpose choice. Many of the disappointments you've experienced and the regrets you still harbor likely have to do with the way that you weren't equal to the moment as a person. You had the talent—but fled. You knew what the next right thing was to do—but blinked. You had the intuition not to open that door—but opened it anyway.

Now you can be different. You can be calm enough to tackle hard subjects. You can be engaged enough to enrich the moment with your full presence. You can be passionate enough to light a fire under your intimate relationship. You can be peaceful enough to take bad news in a more centered way. You can be optimistic enough to handle meaning vanishing for an hour. You can choose to become an upgraded you.

CHAPTER 44

CLASSIC CHOICES: ETHICAL ACTION

S ome people decide that it is important to them to be a good person. It would be lovely if everyone made this choice, but unfortunately many people can't quite see setting the bar that high. Deny our own interests? Deny our desires? Deny our cravings? Deny ourselves conquests and victories? Why?

It can go a bit against the grain to make ethical action a life purpose choice. Human beings tend to be a little too self-interested and ego-driven to really want to go that far. Do we really want to stop everything and read the fine print on the three bins in front of us, so as to meticulously determine where our used hamburger wrapper ought to go? Or are we much more inclined to throw that wrapper in the nearest bin?

And do we really want to debate with ourselves about the morality of eating that hamburger? How complicated this all is! Wouldn't every single choice we try to make involve us in some ethical paradox, conflict, or dilemma—especially if we looked too closely? Isn't life hard enough without such self-pestering? And how could we possibly know enough? Nuclear energy? Vaccines? Mandatory minimum prison sentences? And on and on!

Maybe doing the right thing feels good sometimes. But doing the right thing all the time? Doesn't that seem drastic and impossible, maybe even counter-evolutionary? And who even knows what the right thing is? Haven't we come to understand just how relativistic morality is? If my culture does things one way and your culture does things another way—who's to say? Who's the arbiter of ethics? You? Me? A priest? A rabbi? An imam?

And life shifts. What may seem right to us today about how to handle our parents' healthcare issues, some tricky situation at work, or our own alcohol or drug use may not seem so right to us tomorrow. The situation may have changed. Our own views may have changed. Maybe we have some new insights or new information. Maybe everything has changed!

Plus, sometimes the next right thing to do is a very big thing indeed. Maybe it's an intervention, where we confront our spouse about his or her drinking. Maybe it's leaving our well-paying job because we've learned too much about its overseas practices. Maybe it's leaving the religious order of which we are a member—an action that amounts to leaving our home and family—because the community is not living up to its values. These are huge, life-changing matters. No wonder that we might feel inclined to look the other way!

Plus, sometimes we just want to be bad. Let's admit that. There's a trickster in our pocket and an imp on our shoulder, and that is human nature. Maybe we relish that our friend is getting divorced. Not very nice of us! But there it is. Maybe we want to celebrate our competitor going bankrupt. Not very nice of us! But there it is. Maybe we refrain from telling the cashier that she gave us too much change. Ah, well. Looks like we are human!

And is it more moral to write a plaintive song than a pop song? Doesn't a pop singer deserve to make a living? Is it more moral to represent tenants than to represent landlords? Is every landlord immoral by definition? Is it okay to run an immoral business if we then donate a lot of the profits we make to charity? Is it immoral to will one of our children more money than our other children? Headache time!

All of this makes ethical action a dynamic, never-ending...let's call it opportunity, rather than terrible burden. Every moment, we are presented with the opportunity to try. Maybe we can hold that as a beautiful thing, as the way that the universe wants to test us and to make good use of us, if the universe is into that sort of pursuit.

Or maybe we can just call all this freedom. That's how a fervent existentialist would look at it. Maybe we can simply hold it as one of our prime life purposes choices, to be a good person and to do the next right thing, to the best of our abilities. Remember, we are choosing, so we could make that choice.

There is no guarantee that life will feel more meaningful if we do the next right thing—but it may. Doing the next right thing may even make us happier and physically healthier. But even if none of those benefits accrue, we may still be inclined to choose ethical action as a life purpose choice simply because it strikes us as the right thing to do. Living according to our values may just strike us as important.

CHAPTER 45

COMBINING LIFE PURPOSES: CREATIVITY AND ACTIVISM

So far, I've been describing life purposes as separate things. However, they can also go together beautifully. Career, excellence, and self-actualization can all be pursued at the same time. Service, compassion, and presence can reinforce one another. A great example of this is how the combination of activism and creativity, when they are pursued together, can prove to be a rich life purpose choice.

You can be an activist and you can be creative, and you might keep those pursuits separate. Many creatives do. But you could also integrate them. Here's one example. In 1832, Angelina Grimké, the daughter of an aristocratic, slave-holding Southern family, became an abolitionist as a matter of conscience. Publicly championing the unpopular abolitionist cause constituted an act of engagement and an example of conscience in action.

In 1835, Angelina converted her older sister Sarah to the cause of abolishing slavery, and together they became the first women to speak in public for Black enslaved persons, and, later, for women's rights. They became founding activists in two life-affirming civil rights movements. As activists, they persuaded their mother to give them legal ownership of the enslaved people who constituted their share of the family estate, whom they immediately freed.

Then, in part as a testament to their Quaker faith, they began making speeches and lecturing against slavery in New York and New England, speaking at engagements that included Angelina's three effective appearances before the Massachusetts legislative committee on antislavery petitions in 1838. In addition, among other nonfiction pieces, Sarah wrote *An Epistle to the Clergy of the Southern States* (1836), urging abolition, and *Letters on the Equality of the Sexes and the Condition of Woman* (1838). Angelina wrote *An Appeal to the Christian Women of the South* (1836).

Standing up for abolition constituted engagement; speaking out made them activists; and quietly sitting and dealing with the challenges involved in writing effective nonfiction made them activist artists. Creating something that could move a listener by virtue of its rhetorical strength constituted an act of engaged creativity. Isn't that a beautiful marrying of two life purpose choices? And don't we suppose that these two brave sisters experienced many moments of meaning over the course of their efforts?

A musician who attends a rally is engaged. If he helps organize the rally, he is an activist. When he composes a song for the cause and then plays it at the rally, both the composition and the performance are acts of engaged creativity. They are acts that require that he make use of his talents, skills, mind, heart, hands, and personal presence in ways that are different from—not better than or more courageous than, but different from—how he engages when he signs a petition, writes a check to fund a good cause, or builds a barricade.

In exactly the same sense, a physician who travels to Africa without pay to provide medical services for the indigent poor is engaged and an activist. But if he discovers upon his arrival that he must invent new procedures because of conditions on the ground, that situational need demands that he engage the creative part of his nature, the part that innovates and dreams up new combinations. Both the protest song and the new medical procedure are acts of engaged creativity: that is, *creative effort in service to ethical purposes.*

The phrase "art and activism" is the common term used to convey these ideas. "Art and activism" refers to activities as diverse as the following: the sociopolitical street theater of the San Francisco Mime Troupe;

the activities of the Guerrilla Girls in support of female visual artists; a Bolivian community-based theater group publicizing the issue of the privatization of water; the performance art of Suzanne Lacy tackling issues like rape and aging; Thousand Kites, a storytelling project about the criminal-justice system; and countless more.

Creative people who opt to make use of their creativity in the service of their ethics sometimes actually do make a difference. Like Harriet Beecher Stowe, they may produce a book like *Uncle Tom's Cabin* that moved the war against slavery forward. They may write a book like *1984* that alerts tens of millions of readers to creeping totalitarianism. They may paint as Goya painted and make the world look firing squads in the eye.

Are these results too small? On a human-sized scale, they surely are not. Think about the contours of your own life and consider integrating creativity with activism and becoming an engaged artist. Creativity and activism are each classic life purpose choices on their own, each a rich purpose in its own right. Together, they can amount to something truly special.

CHAPTER 46

SECOND CHOOSING

Earlier, you created your first list of life purpose choices. Then I invited you to think about a score of classic life purpose choices, choices like love and intimacy, family and parenting, health and well-being, work and career, and so on. Some of those were no doubt completely familiar to you, and were perhaps already on your list. Others may have surprised you, opened your eyes a bit, and struck you as worth thinking about further. Now, I'd like to give you the chance to hit pause and consolidate.

I'm guessing that some curiosity may have percolated up in response to ideas like experimentation, appreciation, ethical action, etc.; the idea of combining choices (like creativity and activism); the idea that you can adopt states of being as life purpose choices (including states such as calmness, passion, thoughtfulness, or self-confidence); and so on. This is your opportunity to think about them further.

Consider the classic life purpose choices I presented. Did one or more of them resonate for you? Can the ones that resonated simply be added to your current list of life purpose choices, or do you need to modify your list in some way, combining, subtracting, or altering some choices? Maybe you identified a choice one way and I described it a different way. Spend some time with the array of classic life purpose choices that I just presented and let them infiltrate your consciousness.

Second, to ensure that you aren't leaving anything important out of your considerations, make a separate list of "everything that's important to me or might conceivably be important to me." As before, when you were doing your first choosing, try not to censor yourself. Anything might appear on your list: spending more time with the cat; traveling to Paris to see if that jazz club still exists; going through your grandmother's letters with an eye to writing a novel; giving your brother one more chance; apples, oranges, pears, and strawberries—anything at all.

Let yourself be surprised and intrigued. Where did that one come from? What can that possibly mean? Traveling to Paris to see if that jazz club still exists? What's that about? Spending more time with the cat? Seriously? Ah, and my grandmother's letters. That is complicated. That feels like a place of pressure, the pressure to "do" something with them, a place of love and honor, and a dozen other tangled things as well. I guess I had better sit with that a bit and try to tease that apart...

Next, give yourself the following instruction: try to discern where each choice is "coming from." Is this one ego-driven? Is that one coming from loneliness? Is this one someone else's idea of what's important? Which are the ones that feel most value-driven, propelled by some sense of principled living? Which are the ones that feel necessary to balance out your life, that is, needed because they're supportive of other choices? Which are the ones that feel just a little suspicious or off in some way?

It isn't that one source is "better" than another source. Maybe activism and service are driven by values, excellence and achievement driven by ego, family and parenting driven by love, and work and career driven by survival needs. They can all live together! You're not trying to determine which are the ethical choices in order to strike all the other ones off your list—not at all. What you are doing is trying to discern if any of your choices are coming from some shadowy place that you yourself want to reject. Is a given choice perhaps coming from a place of meanness and revenge? Well, if so, that's your choice—but are you happy with that choice?

It would be lovely if you remained mindful of your values and decided to live an ethical life. That would be good for all of us. It would be wonderful if you lived by the phrase "do the next right thing" and if you lived out what it clearly signifies. But you are the arbiter of all such matters. Love, which isn't "ethical," may matter to you. Excellence, which isn't "ethical," may matter to you. Peacefulness, which isn't "ethical," may matter to you. Create the life that makes sense to you, keeping one eye on ethics but keeping both eyes on the big picture.

The whole picture is the key. A given choice, standing alone, may come with a question mark. But in context, as part of your complete program for living, it may have its rightful place and make perfect sense. Seen in isolation, watching that one television series for an hour each day may seem a little trivial or even unworthy. But as the thing you do after six hours of ethical action, well, then it fits, as something not only appropriate but maybe even necessary. It isn't important by itself, but it is important in context.

Having done the above work, it would be a fine thing if you now possessed a clear picture of how you intend to live your life. That would be delightful! But not to worry if you aren't in the clear yet. We have a "third choosing" coming in a bit, after we've looked at some challenges that need to be addressed. So, no need to worry if your list doesn't feel complete or finished yet. Another reckoning is coming! For now, relax, enjoy, and congratulate yourself on the work you're doing.

CHAPTER 47

CHALLENGE I: THE ELEPHANT IN THE ROOM

Earlier, I presented four scenarios of folks engaged in life purpose choosing. I could have presented many, many more, as many scenarios as there are human beings. And in many of those scenarios, we would see the following: that some overarching, pressing life purpose dominates. It is the big deal thing, the thing most on that person's mind and in their heart.

Maybe it's your love of animals and your life as a vet. Everything is organized around animals. Maybe it's your driving desire to make it as an actor, to get the best roles, to get any roles, to cozy up to A-listers, and at the same time to get as much sex, drugs, and attention as possible. Maybe it's an abiding sense of purpose that has expressed itself in a life as a rural doctor, where everything is organized around you serving your underserved community.

If your current life purpose choosing is done against the backdrop of some big thing like that, some "elephant in the room" of that size, then of course whatever you contemplate as a possible life purpose choice is going to be held up against that measure: "Will this have a negative impact on my vet practice?" "Is that helping me get the roles I want?" "Does this choice serve my patients?"

Having a child, taking a vacation, spending more time with your spouse—everything and anything is measured against that one thing, and is often tabled in light of its effects on that organizing principle. Indeed, is this even life purpose choosing? If nothing is important enough to break the chains of that main thing, are we even entitled to call them "important"? Or are they really secondary, or ancillary? Or not even important at all?

Can you really embark on life purpose choosing if there is an elephant in the room, if something is so central to your life that everything else is measured against it—and is typically found wanting? Won't that elephant prevent growth, change, healing, or even love? Or...is the elephant really all you want out of life? Maybe it's animals and nothing else? An Academy Award and nothing else? Alcohol and nothing else?

Well, the proof is in the pudding and in the living. As a rule, in real life, organizing your life around "just one thing" doesn't play out well. As an example, the suicide rate among police officers is dramatically highest in the five years before retirement. For them, there is a tremendous agony in contemplating the loss of that "one big thing." When everything is measured against just one thing—when your feelings of self-worth rise and fall according to how that elephant is doing—life tends not to work.

Beethoven organized his life around music; Van Gogh organized his life around painting; Virginia Woolf organized her life around writing; and they each struggled mightily with the vicissitudes of life. The great inventor Nikola Tesla organized his life around inventing one amazing thing after another, from the Tesla coil to the laser, and wandered the streets of Manhattan every night in his state of discontent. In real life, living for that elephant is not the way to live.

So, if this is you, here is a question to ask yourself: "Is organizing my life around just one life purpose really a good idea?" Ask it as a real question, not a rhetorical one. You don't want your answer to be a reflexive and automatic "Yes!" You want some real freedom to consider the matter. That elephant has a lot of weight; see if you can keep it weightless for at least as long as it takes to really consider your best interests.

You might discover that letting in love and intimacy are good ideas—and not just love of animals, or music, or the best roles, or inventing. You might discover that your emotional health also matters, and that existing in despair much of the time is not a great way to live. You might discover that it's time to let go of how much you "love Scotch" or "love intrigues" or "love shopping." What else might you discover?

Take a genuine step to the side, out of the elephant's shadow and into the sunshine of this present moment and some clear thinking. That is part of the process of life purpose choosing, dealing with the possibility—and maybe the reality—that you have organized your life around "one big thing," and that maybe doing so wasn't such a brilliant idea. Take a good look at that.

CHAPTER 48

CHALLENGE II: MANY TOO-SMALL PURPOSES

S ay that you've done the work so far, acquainted yourself with all sorts of classic life purpose choices, took a deep dive into your inner self, and did the work of identifying what's important to you, then translated that information into a list of actionable life purposes. Excellent! But... possibly you've arrived at the following challenging place.

Maybe you've come face-to-face with the knowledge that all of your life purpose choices, as much as you want to invest in them and take them seriously, just feel small and only marginally important to you. You keep trying to call them really and truly important, but they just don't feel that way. That is not a good feeling or a good place to land.

It will not work that well to try to say, "I am making this unimportant-feeling thing one of my life purpose choices." Nor will it work very well to try the following gambit: "Okay, none of my choices feels particularly important, but at least I've got a lot of them, so maybe in the aggregate they can feel important? Maybe all of these relatively unimportant-feeling life purpose choices can add up to a way of life that feels purposeful?"

Sounds doubtful, doesn't it? What might help? Well, perhaps the 'smallness' of a choice can be seen in a larger context. For instance, substituting blueberries for potato chips as your afternoon snack may not strike you as wildly important. But if you've designated "physical health" as a life purpose choice and this substitution supports that choice, it really isn't that trivial. You might begin to say to yourself, "This small thing isn't really that small, seen in context."

In the same vein, you might want to think through whether several of your current choices can be gathered together and combined into a single, larger life purpose choice. For instance, maybe you've put studying French, watching physics videos, and taking a watercolor class onto your life purposes list; and maybe each of those feels just too small for you to really care about. But if you notice their relatedness and rename your life purpose choice as "lifelong learning," that newly minted life purpose choice might have the range and significance to inspire you.

Or maybe there is a useful conversation you can have with yourself where you address what may be a self-esteem issue that is making your life purpose choices feel small. It's possible that because you think of yourself as small, you naturally characterize all of the choices you make as also being small. "Why should I care about my health, if I don't care about myself?" "Why should I care about my creativity, if I don't care about myself?" "Why should I care about having love in my life, if I don't care about myself?"

Now, instead, you might say, "I am not small." Then you might say, "Therefore, my choices are not small." You may have to have this conversation with yourself many times over and in many different ways. One conversation may sound like, "I am not made small by my chronic illness. My health condition is real, but it hasn't made me small!" Another might sound like, "Yes, I've disappointed myself in a hundred different ways, but that was yesterday and the day before, and none of that has shrunk me."

Ah, but maybe you're inclined to reject this whole project of life purpose choosing. Your reasoning might go something like this: "If all I'm doing is nominating this and that as my life purposes, how valid or important is that? Isn't that just me playing a pointless game? All I'm doing is saying that nothing really matters and it's all just trying to plug that huge leak with some improvised meaning. Better to be lazy or indulgent or anything at all, rather than play that absurd game!"

You can see that there is an even worse place to land than feeling that your life purpose choices feel like they're on the small side. That worse place to land is the feeling that nothing feels important at all. There are many variations on this theme of rejection. Some are angrier; some are more despairing. Some are more anxious, and some are more ironic. Each is tremendously painful. It is terrible to arrive at a place of concluding that nothing feels important at all.

We must face that dreadful possibility, which for millions is an actuality. Maybe you've completely lost your appetite for life. Maybe you respond to all of your own enthusiasms with "Who cares?" and "That doesn't matter!" Maybe nothing generates that certain feeling, the feeling of meaning. That is a crisis that must be addressed. Let's go there next.

CHAPTER 49

CHALLENGE III: NO PURPOSES AT ALL

We can talk ourselves into the belief that life matters just as we can talk ourselves into the belief that life doesn't matter. We can announce that our health is important to us, or we can say, "Nothing is important to me." We can take action to fulfill our lifelong dreams of writing a novel or wandering around Europe, eating and daydreaming, or we can say, "Nothing matters to me." It's all entirely up to you.

You know where I would like you to land. I would like you to land on the side of appetite, energy, desire, ethics, self-authorship, instrumentality, caring, and life itself. I would like you to have feelings of importance rise up in you. Can you generate those feelings by wanting them and by willing them into existence? That's the question. If you've arrived at the place where you can't identify anything that feels important to you or where you feel that creating your set of life purposes is rather an empty gesture, you have that question to answer.

Do you want aspects of your life to feel important? Do you want life to matter? Maybe you've concluded: "No, who cares about my life purposes—me included. Why bother with these phony life purposes that I've elevated to some high-and-mighty place? Life is too hard, intractable, and pointless for that. Acting like I have 'life purposes' is pathetic!" If so, you know what I am asking you to do. I am asking you to change your mind.

Our emotional health and our existential well-being depend on us making our own life purpose choices. Of course, we understand the power of the other side, the nihilistic side, and how a belief that nothing matters can rob us of enthusiasm and make us doubt the value of life purpose choosing. Well, what then?

Let us recognize that this rejection of the idea of self-created life purpose choices is a hangover from the belief that life should be meaningful in some other deeper and more important sense. Life shouldn't just be organized around some purposes that you get to name, this hangover belief goes, it should have a specific innate purpose. We quite understand this hangover pull to reject the exact truth of the matter, which is that we ourselves must decide what's important.

You can and must learn to accept that you intend to live a life based on your own calculations, even though the universe doesn't care one way or the other. Likewise, you can and must learn how to respond to the truth that life is exactly like this. What will your rejoinder be? "I don't need the cosmos to care. I care!" Or: "I may just be excited matter, but I quite enjoy mattering!" Or: "Every one of my life purposes makes perfect sense to me!"

You can even revel in the enterprise of naming and living your life purposes. Which of my life purposes shall I live today? Ah, what excellent choices! To love, to create, to serve, to right a wrong, to gain some mastery, to explore; what a lovely day! You reject that pair of impertinent questions, "What is the meaning of life?" and "What is the purpose of life?" and you strive to answer the only really pertinent question, "How do I intend to live?" You shift the paradigm through your own individual action.

A major obstacle can arise when we do not find any way to ground ourselves in a felt sense of purpose. It's possible you may be missing a certain feeling—the feeling of meaning—and come to believe that life is empty and pointless in reaction. It is abundantly clear that we crave that feeling. Human beings crave that feeling of meaning more than they crave sex, Scotch, or peanut butter. Of course, we want that feeling! Just as we want feelings like joy and happiness in our life, we want feelings of meaning.

We would prefer life to feel meaningful rather than meaningless, just as we would prefer life to feel joyful rather than despairing. Of course, we do! That feeling is motivating. It helps us do our work, whatever our work may be. When something we are doing feels meaningful, well, it feels meaningful! And when something we are doing feels meaningless, well, we are not much motivated to do it. So, yes, we crave that feeling! But despite the power of such cravings, we must talk ourselves down from that desire.

We can learn to watch out for the quite reasonable, quite natural, and quite disturbing thought that our life purpose choices are merely insignificant personal selections and not as valid as something cosmically ordained. At the same time, we finally—perhaps for the first time—arrive at a clear picture of what "meaning" is and why it so important that we reduce its significance in our life. Let me explain.

CHAPTER 50

THE WRONG QUESTION

If I were to ask you, "Is life joyful?" you would immediately see the problem with that question. You would simply answer, "Sometimes," and "It depends." But if I were to ask you, "Is life meaningful?" you would suddenly get very fuzzy. You likely wouldn't know how to answer it. The question might even throw you into a bit of a tizzy.

That's because the question "Is life meaningful?" is really demanding that you answer a very different question: "Is the universe purposeful and, if it is, in what sense?" That's what that question, framed in that way, demands by way of an answer. It asks you to provide an answer to the question, "What does the universe want?" Of course, not only don't you know the answer, but you can sense the unfairness and absurdity of that question. What does the universe want? Are you kidding me?

"Is life meaningful?" is a frankly unfair question. It isn't asking you about yourself, which is a subject you know something about. It isn't asking, "What do you experience as meaningful?" which may be a difficult question to answer but is at least a fair question. No, it is asking you to explain the universe. How patently absurd!

Once you recognize the unfairness and absurdity of the question, "Is life meaningful?" you can begin to ask yourself the much fairer question, "How does this thing called 'meaning' operate in my life?" And what you will discover is that meaning is just a feeling! This is a breathtaking bit of news. To sum it up: purpose is a choice, and meaning is a feeling.

Your life purposes are choices. But meaning is just a feeling. It is a feeling that we can try to coax into existence (we'll call this activity "making meaning"), and it is certainly a feeling that we want, but as "just a feeling," its place in your life recedes dramatically. How important is a feeling on a scale of one to ten? Just middling. If you organize your life around your life purposes and let meaning take care of itself—let it come when it wants to come, and let it go when it decides to go—you are all set!

This is the second paradigm shift that I'm suggesting you embrace. The first was the shift from the idea that "life has a purpose, and it is predefined" to the idea that you are obliged to choose your life purposes—in the plural. This second paradigm shift is likewise easy to say: it is the shift from seeking meaning as if it were something to uncover or capture to making meaning; to the idea that the feeling of meaning is yours to try to generate.

Once you make this transition, you'll begin to hear yourself say, "Oh, I see. It isn't that a sunset, a Buddhist text, a baby's smile, a promotion at work, winning the Pulitzer Prize, or helping an old lady across the streets are intrinsically meaningful in themselves. I might not experience any of that as personally meaningful. Things are not intrinsically meaningful—they are either experienced as meaningful or they aren't experienced that way. Wow. That's interesting."

Your next thought might be: "Well, and what does that imply? Maybe it suggests that what I am after is the psychological experience of meaning. But how do I create, conjure up, or chase this experience? How do I know what to try? How do I know what to do? What is this strange activity of trying to produce experiences of meaning? Or could it be that the task might be a completely different one? Is it possible that what's wanted is simply to no longer need those experiences? That's interesting. What if I were to say to myself, 'Struggling to create experiences of meaning is actually a waste of my time. Let me just live.' Might that work?"

See where we're heading? This hints at two different sorts of answers to "the problem of meaning." One is to learn how to create, invite into existence, or otherwise conjure up experiences of meaning (which we'll call "making meaning," though it is more like coaxing than making). The other is to announce that such experiences are rather beside the point. And maybe these two ideas can be combined into a very simple-to-say (if not simple-to-live) program: "I will endeavor to make meaning without, at the same time, caring all that much about meaning."

But...if I'm no longer caring that much about meaning, what am I in fact caring about? To repeat: purpose. You decide to care about your life purposes. You affirm, "Living my life purposes is more important to me than chasing the experience of meaning." You tie that to the idea of "value" and massage that statement a bit: "Living my value-based life purposes is more important to me than chasing the experience of meaning." That is a life-changing mouthful.

CHAPTER 51

WHEN MEANING VANISHES

Let me repeat and underline the point that I just made: meaning comes and goes. That is how we are built, and it should therefore stop surprising us. It should stop surprising us that something that once felt meaningful no longer does. It should no longer surprise us that a big investment that we decide to make, say in pursuing an advanced college degree, does not feel meaningful as we do it. None of that should surprise us any longer.

It should no longer surprise us that the psychological experience of meaning can vanish in an instant. Think of a feeling like happiness. Can't happiness be wiped out in a moment? Of course, it can. Something bad happens—a medical diagnosis, an accident befalling your child—and your happiness vanishes. You were happy the moment before—now you are not. The same is true for meaning.

If you aren't alert to this reality, you may feel supremely disconcerted that "the meaning of life" can disappear just like that. Where did meaning go? Well, it went away, just as happiness or joy or anger or any other feeling can and does depart. We understand this when it comes to joy; we seem not to understand it when it comes to meaning, perhaps because meaning "feels different." Now we are ready to embrace this reality!

If you do recognize this, you will be swayed and confused far less often. Say that you are attending a talk given by a well-known rabbi, Indian mystic, or New Age spiritual leader. His voice is comforting; his delivery is seamless. His demeanor seems grounded and centered. You experience your time there as meaningful. The event is evoking that certain feeling.

Then, right as you are leaving, you overhear two women talking about the speaker's predatory nature. It turns out that he is a well-known pedophile. There goes your feeling of meaning, just like that, vanished in an instant! How you interpret that loss is important. If you are still laboring under the belief that meaning is a feeling, you're likely to feel deceived, conned, and drawn in by this practiced conman—duped and bereft of positive feelings. But if you hold meaning in the way described here, you can say with ease, "Wow, listening to him felt meaningful. I'm glad such feelings don't matter that much!"

If you are actively living your life purposes, then if by chance listening to such a celebrity huckster did provoke feelings of meaning within you, which then vanished when you learned the truth about him, you would know that all that had happened was that you felt something, but now you don't—which you now understand is no big deal. Nothing gigantic happened!

If you believe meaning to be something "out there" and think of it as something that must be searched for because it resides outside of yourself, then every event of this sort will disturb and demoralize you and maybe even seriously harm you. Life will keep betraying you. Feeling betrayed, there you will find yourself again, lost in the tangled wilderness of pining for meaning.

Once you understand that the feeling of meaning comes and goes—that its mere presence does not signify anything spectacular and its absence is nothing tragic—then you will have put life on a solid footing. You will not freeze up in distress when a hero turns out to have feet of clay; nor will you feel your world crumble when a lover leaves town. Instead, you will be able to say in such instances, "Back to the project of my life, doing the next right thing and deciding for myself what's important."

Painful events will still sting; this updated and upgraded understanding of life, with its focus away from meaning and toward instrumentality, will not provide a complete cure or full immunity from suffering. But it is bound to make a real difference!

Imagine investing in that guru to the extent of following him to Nepal and joining his dogmatic community, in contrast to smiling to yourself as you listen to him and whispering to yourself, "He sounds good, he's even giving me a feeling of specialness, but as soon as this lecture is over, back to my life purposes!" What a misadventure you would have saved yourself!

CHAPTER 52

THE DOUBLE WHAMMY

Let's take a more dramatic example. It is one thing if meaning vanishes. That is just a feeling disappearing. It is another thing, and much more serious, if what vanishes with it is our sense of purpose. That's a powerful double whammy that produces the deepest crises. It is one thing for meaning to vanish. But if its absence suddenly makes you doubt the importance of the thing you are doing, that is a major, even life-altering event.

Consider the following. You enter a graduate program with high hopes, excitement, and enthusiasm. You feel you are on what you are internally calling a meaningful path. Looking at the description of the classes feels exciting—those descriptions generate that certain feeling. The program "feels meaningful." You can't wait to get started, you find yourself in a good mood (because experiences of meaning elevate mood), you splurge on a new computer, you sharpen your pencils, and you practically sing your way to your first classes.

You begin your program—and none of your classes meet your expectations. One is taught by a bully; one is dull and detail-oriented. One makes no sense to you, and another is flat-out boring. In none of these classes do you experience the feeling of meaning.

If you're not used to the concept of meaning as a feeling, you may not be able to brush all this off and say to yourself, "It looks like these classes aren't going to provide me with the experience of meaning. Maybe getting my degree is still a valuable idea for certain reasons, but I see that the program is not going to feel very meaningful or meet my need for meaning." Rather than speaking to yourself that way, you're likely to say, "This is so depressing" and "I think I ought to quit." A real crisis is occurring!

Suddenly you no longer believe in either the field of study or the profession. Not only has meaning vanished, so has purpose. The subject matter no longer seems important. You thought that your studies would feel more special—that cognitive science would have more interesting things to say about consciousness than it appears to have, that art history would feel like an adventure more like going to Florence than merely learning names and dates, or that clinical psychology would be more about human nature than it appears to be.

You suddenly "see through" your chosen profession and have no idea what to do next. You've taken out loans and you have no alternative plan; you're apparently committed to this path, and yet you hate where you are. What naturally follows? You begin to skip classes and procrastinate on assignments. You find yourself unable to sleep as your mind pesters you with thoughts like "How can I make this better?" and "These classes are so awful!" and "Should I drop out?" and "If I drop out, what will I do with my life?"

For the first time in your life, you experience serious insomnia. You also find that you have no appetite, which mirrors your loss of appetite for life, and you find yourself losing significant weight. On many days, you find it hard to get out of bed. This is a scenario of one typical meaning crisis and the predictable rhythms that would ensue. Nothing happened "clinically" speaking: your brain did not suddenly become disordered. What happened was exactly the following: you invested meaning in the idea of something, and its reality badly disappointed you, and the experience therefore failed to provide you either with experiences of meaning or a workable way to maintain this life purpose choice.

What our graduate student might wisely do is one of the following two things. First, she might try to reinvest in her life purpose of becoming a professional of a certain sort (a cognitive scientist, an art historian, or a psychologist in the above examples), hold her nose, make it through her classes, and find other ways to coax some meaning into existence even while feeling her program is devoid of meaning. That is, she might still be able to hold her professional goal as important even if her graduate studies feel meaningless.

Alternatively, she might catch her breath, announce that her professional choice no longer makes sense to her, and refuse to bad-mouth herself about "abandoning her program," "being a quitter," or "making a tragic mistake." She might then either plot a new course, or, if it is too soon for that, take a needed break. She might announce that for a period of time, she won't be hunting for meaning or even concerning herself with the need for meaning. She might allow herself to relax.

She will also likely need to do some forgiving: she will need to forgive herself for having been seduced by this shiny path, as well as the universe for cheating her out of that path. If she drops both her graduate studies and her chosen profession, two crises will have occurred, a crisis of meaning and a crisis of purpose. That is a lot. Meaning's propensity to come and go is one thing. The fact that when it vanishes, it can take our sense of purpose with it is a graver thing and a crisis that must be weathered.

CHAPTER 53

CHALLENGE IV: STRANGELY IMPORTANT

We've seen how a life can either consciously or inadvertently come to be organized around one big life purpose, with the result that other valuable life purposes may be strenuously excluded. We've also seen how a life may be organized around many "small" life choices, leaving the person feeling not quite satisfied or fulfilled. Now let's look at a true oddity: the way in which human beings often designate this or that as what can only be called "strangely important."

As an analogy, think of the kind of real estate shows where prospective buyers visit home after home, looking for a home to buy. The wife will tell the real estate agent, "It must have a bathtub;" the husband will announce to the real estate agent, "It must have a view of the sea." They visit a house that meets *all* their criteria for ideal living—but it doesn't have a bathtub, so it is rejected. The next house is perfect! But it doesn't have a view of the sea—rejected! What is going on here?

What is happening is something seriously human. Human beings get it into their heads that their hoped-for life must include a wraparound porch, or dual vanities in the bathroom, or stainless-steel appliances, or quartz kitchen countertops. How can the absence of dual vanities be more important than everything else being perfect? Because of human nature.

You identify as a short story writer. Your dream, which is never far from your mind, is to be published in the *New Yorker*. You get published in many places, and two collections of your short stories come out. But the *New Yorker* never publishes you—so you consider yourself a failure. Isn't that strange? You have had real successes, more successes than ninety-nine out of a hundred short story writers—but you can't get over falling short of the mark with the *New Yorker*.

You work in a large corporation and have wended your way into upper management. But that really important person in the corner office has never invited you to join him and his buddies for a round of golf. You've taken golf lessons and bought the best clubs, and you keep pining for the invitation...which just doesn't come. People see you as a success, yet you see yourself as a failure. Isn't that completely strange?

This is something like a hypnotic trance, isn't it? Human nature has primed us to fall into peculiar trances of this sort, where we feel miserable if we are never published by the *New Yorker* no matter how well we do otherwise, or miserable if we're never invited to play golf with the boss, even though that's the last thing we may actually want to do.

Part of the process of life purpose choosing is breaking any trances that may currently have you hypnotized. But how do you do that? How is that even possible? How can someone under a hypnotic spell snap her own fingers and end the trance? Well, let's try it. You are hypnotized. But you are also free not to be hypnotized. Snap your fingers! Just snap your fingers. Let's see if you can free yourself, just like that.

Maybe you won't notice a difference after that finger snap. But maybe you will. Maybe the *New Yorker* is suddenly just not very important to you. Maybe that round of golf with your boss is suddenly just not very important to you. Perhaps you have just freed yourself from that strange trance, one that had no real rhyme or reason. If so, congratulations!

If not, maybe you've at least grown in awareness. Possibly unhooking yourself from that hypnotic sense of attachment will happen soon. Part of the process of life purpose choosing is unhooking yourself from whatever may be only strangely important, as opposed to that which is *genuinely* important. Here's to that process of self-liberation!

It may be genuinely important that your new house have enough bedrooms for all the kids—and not important at all that it have quartz countertops in the kitchen. Bedrooms? Yes. Quartz countertops? No. Free of huge structural issues? Yes. Dual vanities? No. Let any and all hypnotic trances end now!

CHAPTER 54

CHALLENGE V: FORMERLY IMPORTANT

Say that you've chosen reading as a life purpose choice and a meaning opportunity. You've enjoyed reading mystery novels in the past, but for this or that reason, you haven't picked one up in a while. So, as the concrete expression of your new life purpose choice to read, you get your hands on a mystery novel.

Will you still have a taste for mysteries? Will the one you pick up hold your attention? Will it prove a pleasure? Who can say? You can only know by trying. You make an investment in this experience by locating a novel, finding a quiet spot to read, and reading. But you do not over-invest. You don't put your well-being on the line with this little experiment!

If the experience proves pleasurable, enjoy it! Then bank it: put it in your memory banks as an experience that you actually enjoyed. It is so important to know which of our experiences we've truly liked! Enjoy it and memory bank it; and, of course, schedule it. This has been confirmed as one of your life purposes, and now you get to live it.

If the experience proves neutral or negative, it may amount to a disappointment and, unless you are careful, even a defeat. If this happens, take a step to the side and apply your awareness to the situation. Pause and think. Murmur to yourself, "That was very interesting. I really expected that I would enjoy reading that mystery, and I didn't enjoy it at all. What happened, I wonder?"

It may mean that you can't read mysteries until you get your own mystery written, the one that you've put aside for a year. Maybe mystery-reading pleasure is being held hostage and can't be released until the ransom of your own mystery is paid. For a creative person, that's a likely possibility. Your better life purpose choice may be "write my mystery" rather than "read some mysteries."

It might mean that this particular mystery wasn't very good. It may mean that your tastes have changed, that cozy mysteries are now too lightweight for you and you now need hardboiled mysteries. It may mean that your sleuthing skills have improved and that you landed on the identity of the killer so early in the story that the rest of the mystery felt anticlimactic. How boring to identify the killer by page nine!

It's possible it means that until you attend to your other life purposes, you do not have permission from yourself to relax and be entertained. Maybe there is a cause you are committed to supporting that you've been avoiding. This experience may have alerted you to that. Revisiting what felt important to us in the past is a great way to learn what's important to us now!

Whenever we revisit something that served us in the past, we can't know if it will still serve us. We hope that it will; we have our fingers crossed. If we liked it back then, we would love it if we still like it now. But each such repeat visit is on the order of an experiment in knowing. You identify what you consider important—and then you learn if it is still important to you by penciling it into your calendar.

Many things that once felt important to me no longer do. World travel would have been found high up on any life purposes list of mine from twenty years ago. Now, it hardly makes the list, if it is there at all. Writing fiction would have appeared at the very top of such a list in my twenties; but these days, after sixty books written and published for many and varied reasons, it does not appear at all. Our life purpose choices change!

If you aren't certain whether something still retains its importance, experiment. You may be able to experiment in your mind's eye, without having to actually book an around-the-world trip or start writing a novel. Picture the reality of that trip, or of writing that novel. If what wells up is enthusiasm, that is good to know! But if you find yourself shaking your head in the negative, that too is information.

CHAPTER 55

CHALLENGE VI: CORE DOUBT

I could continue to identify challenges from here to infinity. Among them would be the difficult people in your life; your particular circumstances; your formed personality, ingrained habits, and defensiveness; the mood swings and anxiety you experience; and more. I could go on! Let us just call all of that "life" and counter all such challenges with a fresh pledge to live your life purposes.

But even with your pledge in hand in mind, you may still feel undermined by some core doubt. That core doubt might sound like the following: "Coming up with my own life purposes feels so artificial and so arbitrary. Maybe life really wants something completely different from me than what I've come up with—should I keep poking around, searching, and seeking?"

Or your core doubt might sound like this: "What I want and what I believe in seem to shift all the time. Therefore, isn't it possible there really aren't any such thing as life purposes? Could it be there are only whims, desires, and cravings, and none of it is more substantial than air? Maybe nothing is 'really important'—that seems completely possible and even likely!"

Or that core doubt might sound like: "Human beings are such disposable, self-centered, trivial creatures—what a lot of silly arrogance to talk about life purposes when most people seem to behave more like creatures in the insect world! Imagine bugs talking about their life purposes! What a wonderful Walt Disney movie that would make!"

Or the core doubt you struggle with may sound like: "I am such a slave to my appetites—what a joke to think about life purposes! I can hardly stop myself from eating jar after jar of peanuts or shopping online day and night. Life purposes indeed! I'm nothing but a walking addiction!"

The point is that some default thought may tug at you, seemingly attempting to pull the rug right out from under you. That thought may have its reasons: for instance, if it wins, you won't have to do all the heavy lifting of actually living your life purposes! Then you could discard your long list of life purposes like a spent grocery list. Done with that! Back to watching football or a romantic comedy!

But you can either live your life purposes while harboring a doubt or two, or you can give in to those doubts and, having stood up for a time, sit back down. You know that feeling; you know how it feels to throw up your hands and give up. Standing up for what you really want in life may be exhausting—but isn't the feeling of giving up even worse?

Stand up, please. Raise your fist. Cheer yourself on. Challenges will still be coming; there is no doubt that they are. A virus may lay you low for a month. Your parents may still laugh at your aspirations. That bottle of Scotch may still look very attractive. Strange enthusiasms may still well up in you, causing you to lose track of time as you research the history of ghosts or expat living in Portugal. Keep standing!

In a moment or two, I'll ask you to repeat the process of life purpose choosing, now taking into account the ideas we've covered over the last several chapters. We'll take into account the nature of meaning (and how it comes and goes), the possibility that some of what you previously held as important may no longer strike you that way, and so on. We'll reckon with that in a few moments.

That round of choosing is coming shortly. For now, address any lingering core doubt that keeps coming up. Investigate it, if that seems worthwhile, tease out its reasons, and address those reasons. Or just ask it to leave town. Just tell it that this town isn't big enough for the two of you. Give it the sort of ultimatum that makes a Western movie so satisfying.

CHAPTER 56

VALUE-BASED CHOOSING

What criteria are you using as you make your life purpose choices? Well, one category of criteria is bound to be, "what I value." Yes, this is sort of just another way of saying, "What's important to me." But it has an additional flavor, doesn't it? "What I value" and "what's important to me" are similar, but different.

It may be important to you to run a marathon. But what about running that marathon do you value? Is it "completing a hard thing" or "testing yourself to the limit"? Is it "keeping a promise to yourself," or "keeping a deathbed promise" you made to your father? Is it "showing courage"?

Or the marathon may be important to you—but not for such laudable reasons. There may, in fact, be no value behind it. You may find running a marathon important because it keeps you out of the house and away from domestic disputes. You may find it important because it keeps you fit enough to drink too much. Such unlovely reasons may constitute the underlying rationale.

This is just a brief chat about the difference between "what's important" and "what's valuable." It would be lovely if your life purpose choices were not only important to you but actually reflected your values. To say this awkwardly, we are after value-based life purpose choosing. That is a bit of a mouthful, so can we just call it "value-based choosing"?

It might be important for your ego to get a doctorate in sociology from that grand university and research some arcane corner of group theory. But wouldn't it be more valuable to be of help to some real people? Well, the latter might amount to far more work for far less pay and not satisfy your ego needs very much at all. But would it be of more value?

You can see "the problem with value." That something is valuable doesn't at all mean that it will prove profitable, satisfying, meaningful, or fun. It might prove far more fun to paint a lovely picture of a farm than to run a farm and feed people. Running a farm is such real work! But which is more valuable?

We can certainly find ways of asserting and affirming the value of that prestigious doctorate or that lovely painting. But in a corner of awareness, we know that we are playing a little fast and loose with our definition of value. We are making "value" stand on its head, and that is a hard position to maintain.

I am not suggesting that you should try to become a saint and give over your life to leading "only a life of value." I am not saying to stop painting and plow that field. But I am putting on the table the distinction between value-based life purpose choosing and all other life purpose choosing. When, in our own estimation, a choice really is value based, how good that feels!

This is very tricky territory. If we must do something in order to survive, do we also need to pester ourselves about whether it is or isn't a value-based decision? Do we really have to deconstruct the phrase "art has value," or are we permitted to just let it be? Which is more valuable, to defend the innocent or to prosecute the guilty? Golly!

Let us put this subject off to one side, not to table it but to let it simmer, percolate, and gestate. We do want our life purpose choices to reflect our values. At the same time, this is such a tricky and even a sticky matter! Maybe you might like to revisit your life purposes menu with these new thoughts in mind? Or perhaps you'd just as soon sleep on it.

CHAPTER 57

OPENING TO NEW CHOICES

You made your first list of life purpose choices before encountering many classic life purpose choices. Then you returned to your life purpose choices list and engaged in a second round of choosing. You have just learned about certain challenges that might arise, including challenges connected to meaning, value, and doubt. Next, I'll invite you to try your hand at a third round of choosing, one that takes all of the above into account.

But first, there may be some new life purpose choices wanting to bubble up. Some of your life purpose choices will feel very familiar to you, even all too familiar. There's dieting again; there's exercise again. Some, like returning to a long-tabled creative project, may feel as if they hark back to the distant past. But others may feel rather brand-new. Maybe the idea of service is new to you, or the possibility of activism. Welcome, new choices!

Do some new choices feel as if they want to percolate up? This may be the case. Just out of conscious awareness, you may be reexamining your life, changing long-held opinions, and coming to some new conclusions about what's important to you in life.

Let's give all of that percolating a chance to bubble up! Quiet your racing mind. Breathe in and out. Maybe give yourself the prompt, "What wants to combine?" or "Is something new right around the corner?" Be easy and relaxed. Something momentous may be coming, something that doesn't require any heavy lifting or forced labor. Just think, "I wonder what might be coming." Open the door, in case it wants to arrive that way. Maybe open a window. Who knows how newness wants to enter!

Maybe you love painting. And you resent how women have been treated. You love the identities of iconoclast, warrior, and activist. Likewise, you embrace the idea of absurd rebellion. You intend to defend and exalt your individuality. Suddenly, this all comes together as "rebel feminist artist." "Rebel feminist artist" is the sort of combination of life purpose choices that might suddenly become prominent in your life. Bam!

Emerging newly as they are, such combinations may feel right as well as unexpected. Unexpected choices can make us a bit anxious. Breathe, calm yourself, and begin to ponder the actions that might go with your new choices. What would living as a rebel feminist artist look like? What would need to change in order for you to live that way? What new attitudes would you need to manifest? What actions and behaviors?

And how might this new piece of your identity and life purpose choice connect to your other life purpose choices? To make a small joke of it, how might a rebel feminist artist diet or exercise? Or would she? If some new combination of life purpose choices arrives, consider it on its own as well as in combination with your other life purpose choices. Maybe your whole landscape will need to change!

Let's imagine another combination life purpose choice. Maybe you find your current profession both boring and too low paying. You know that you have to make "career" a life purpose choice. You also know that you've been suppressing your individuality and your creativity. You are smarter than the work you are currently doing, more creative than the work you are currently doing, and, yes, bolder too. You know you have some boldness in you—somewhere.

Maybe this thinking leads you to a place of "bold, creative entrepreneurship." This isn't precisely a new idea for you, because the prospect of launching out on your own has been on your mind for some time. But it has now combined into a powerful life purpose choice that wants to replace both "career" and "creativity" on your list of life purpose choices. So, "career" and "creativity" get crossed off—and "bold, creative entrepreneur" replaces them. Voila!

Pause now. Take a little time. Open to the possibility that some new life purpose choices, maybe hovering just out of conscious awareness, want to make themselves known to you. Invite them to come forward. Maybe smile. These new life purpose choices may prove eye-opening, exciting, even momentous—not the same old choices! How very invigorating.

CHAPTER 58

THIRD CHOOSING

Welcome to more choosing! I've given you plenty to think about, including what may have been some eye-opening notions about meaning and its place in the overall equation of life. Now, I'd like you to take all the time you need to pull together your thoughts and feelings and come up with a third version of your life purpose choices list. Maybe your second version will remain unchanged; or maybe it will morph dramatically. We shall see!

There is no particular process to use as you engage with this third choosing. Just be open to what we've discussed and consider the challenges I described, among them overinvesting in one choice, harboring formless doubts about the process, or finding that your mosaic of "small" life purposes is not amounting to enough. You have plenty to consider. Give yourself an afternoon, making sure to have snacks handy, and consider providing yourself with a journal prompt like, "I wonder where I've landed," or "How does everything combine?"

While you're engaging with this exercise, let me briefly present a client I'll call Jack. Jack worked at a high-paying job that provided for a materially easy life. But like so many of his colleagues, he felt bored, listless, and empty. Something was missing from his life—or maybe many somethings. He hired me on as his existential wellness coach and we chatted. It perplexed him that he should feel so sad and unsettled, given what a good and privileged life he was leading. What more could a person reasonably want, given all that he had?

I explained my ideas about life purposes versus life purpose, making meaning versus seeking meaning, meaning investments and meaning opportunities, organizing each day around his life purposes, and the other ideas I routinely share with clients. He absorbed those ideas and did the work of investigating what was important to him and how those important things might become his life purpose choices.

Over the course of the coaching, he arrived at four life purpose choices: he decided he would write a certain book meant to serve a currently underserved population; he would spend more time with his wife and teenage daughter; he would get fit; and he would take time off from work to visit distant relatives. These may not sound like earth-shattering choices, but these four together amounted to just the right mix for him and allowed him to organize each day in ways that felt solid, settled, and meaningful.

His mind was engaged: working on the book took care of that. His heart was engaged by spending more time just being with his wife and daughter, along with establishing additional meaningful contact with his extended family. His body was attended to—maybe not at the 100 percent level, but at least to the point where he was a regular presence at his gym three or four times a week. Most importantly, he felt existentially settled: he could honestly say that he was living a life of purpose.

He learned that he did not need to have every moment feel meaningful. That understanding allowed him to sometimes be bored, unengaged, or resistant without pestering himself about "the meaning of life" or wondering why life "suddenly felt meaningless." Now, he knew better. He knew to smile and let the cloud pass on by. Right behind that cloud, the sun was still shining.

It struck him as curious that while nothing exactly life-changing had occurred, his life felt entirely different. He felt settled rather than unsettled, productive rather than unproductive, and engaged rather than disengaged. He realized that doing these "simple" things, while not pining for anything else, amounted to a curiously huge change in his outlook. The fact that he had money was a blessing; but creating a life that matched his values was his own doing. Knowing that made him feel proud and good.

I mention Jack because all of the work that we did together, all of his thinking, considering, and choosing, ultimately landed him on a very short, simple list of life purpose choices. What a modest harvest! You, too, may discover that all of the considering I'm asking you to do will bring you to a similar place of having identified just three, four, or five life purpose choices—which will hopefully make them relatively easy to live!

This, then, is your third choosing opportunity. But, of course, it is not your final choosing. You might switch your mind about your life purposes just as you're walking from the market to your car. You might reorder them as the elevator takes you from the eighth floor to the lobby. Create your list "just for now" rather than looking at it as final, and begin to think about how each of your life purpose choices can be translated into concrete daily actions.

CHAPTER 59

HOW EXACTLY?

Let us imagine that you've arrived at the following place. You've generated a list of the things that are important to you. You've done some thinking about your motivations for choosing these in particular. You think some more, nod your head, and ratify these as your current life purpose choices. Maybe you've got three or five or seven or nine life purpose choices named. What now?

At this point, you will need to explain to yourself how each life purpose choice will be lived. How will "creativity" actually be expressed? Or intimacy, health, service, or parenting? It isn't enough to say, "I'm committed to being more creative." To stop there is to stop too soon.

You must ask yourself, "How exactly?" How exactly am I being creative? How exactly am I adding intimacy to my life? How exactly am I "working on my health"? How exactly do I intend to be of service? How exactly will I improve my parenting skills? How exactly?

Exactly means exactly: human beings tend to keep these matters vague, because as long as they are vague, they obligate us to no work, they take no time, and they require no real commitment. "I intend to be of service" and "I intend to spend four hours a week volunteering at the local emergency infant nursery" are like, well, night and day.

Vague is "Creativity is one of my life purpose choices." Less vague is, "And that means, I want to write." Less vague than that is, "I think it's going to be fiction." Less vague still is, "And by fiction, I mean a novel." Are we there? No, not quite.

A would-be writer could remain in the place of "I intend to write a novel" for decades. That is a common place to hang out, tormented by the desire to write, aware that a life purpose choice is slipping on by, but nevertheless adamantly committed to not even naming that novel.

"How exactly?" That's the ticket! What an eloquent, beautiful question. Let's move forward with that.

You nominate intimacy as a life purpose choice. Just by naming intimacy as a life purpose choice, you may feel yourself softening a little, or maybe starting to feel hopeful. Lovely! But next, you may have to say something to your husband or wife. You may have to ask, "Can we get back into the routine of date nights?" That might be exactly the right question.

Think about how you might move from the vague to the concrete. For example, you could move from "creativity" to "writing fiction" to "writing this particular novel." Or you might refine a life purpose choice of "health" to choosing "better diet, exercise, and an annual physical," and from there to selecting a specific food plan, joining a gym, and scheduling your yearly physical.

Vagueness can serve all sorts of shadowy purposes. It can be our passive way of being aggressive; for example, saying, "I'll call later" instead of at a specific time may translate as, "I'll call when I darn well please! I'm in control here!" Yes, this is very human. Let us be careful here and do an excellent job of moving our life purpose choices from general categories to clear and exact actions to take in order to realize our chosen purposes.

CHAPTER 60

A CURATED WEEK

You've created a list of the important things. For each one, you've stepped to the side, turned on a bright light, and made sure that it belongs. You've checked each of them against your values and principles and tried to discern whether any shadowy motivations may be at play. You've translated each "important thing" into a life purpose choice and moved step-by-step from vagueness to exactness. What now?

Well, it would be a fine thing if you could now prioritize them. But what might that mean in our context? Is health to come "above" creativity? Is activism "more important" than service? Are you to choose which is of greater value, spending time alone with your spouse or spending time alone with your children? What sort of process is rank-ordering life choices? Does that even make sense?

All are important. That was the single criterion, after all! These were all chosen because each is important in your life. Well, let's employ an analogy. You run a beautiful, important art gallery. Each week you put up a new show in one of the main spaces. That space has twelve walls available. That's exactly what you have to work with each week. That's it!

You are the curator of that space, and you must make choices about how many pictures to show, which pictures to show, how to organize them, how to light them, and how to make sense of them. You can't show every painting! That's out of the question. Nor can every painting be the first painting that visitors to the gallery see. One painting gets that prize position. But which?

This is what a gallery owner must do. So, she does it. She completely understands that she might make various choices: instead of alternating red, blue, red, blue, she might sequence pieces red, red, red, blue, blue, blue. Each option has its reasons. Still, she must choose.

This is your task, too. Once you've chosen your life purposes, you must choose again. You must choose how those life purpose choices will fit into your life, day by day and week by week. This is exactly like a gallery owner first choosing the hundred paintings she likes from a given artist, then deciding which twenty to present in a curated show. The other eighty are not lost or missing; they are in the back room, ready and waiting for the next show.

There were two rounds of choosing for her, first choosing the original paintings and then choosing how to display some number of them. You have the same task. You name your life purpose choices, then you decide on how you will live some number of them (or all of them, if that seems humanly possible) this month, this week, today. This curation task is your second choosing task.

You look at your list. You think about your week. You stay real and remember to factor in how you're going to feel after that tooth extraction and what it means that your mother-in-law is visiting for two days. You look at your real week, your real tasks and challenges, your real time available, and your real self. Then you say, "Which goes where?"

You're adamant about getting exercise into the week. You pencil that in. You're equally adamant about getting to the novel you're writing. You pen that in. Spending quality time with your children—where does that fit? Does it fit? Must it be skipped? But you don't want it to be skipped! So? So, you won't cook for your mother-in-law, you'll order in pizza. That gains you two hours—two hours you can spend with the kids!

You navigate the week, and you negotiate what goes into its days. This is what "prioritizing your life purpose choices" looks like. It's a lovely, tricky, elaborate process: how do you fit "calmness" in, where does "passion" go, how do you make sure not to forget about your long-term projects, and what about that sixth life purpose choice that seems not to be getting onto any weekly schedule...and so on. What a delicious process! And at the end of it, a curated week.

CHAPTER 61

MILESTONES DEEP DIVE

You've clearly identified actions associated with your life purpose choices. Excellent! You've got them marked on your calendar. Excellent! You've mindfully curated your week. Excellent! You are now living your life purposes. Excellent! The following question then arises. As you live your life purposes, how will you mark your progress?

First of all, is "making progress" even that important? Do you need to move from "one level of calmness" to "a higher level of calmness," as if everything about life were a ladder? If you've written on your novel every day this week but haven't made much "real progress," should that feel like a defeat? Should we really be so attached to the idea of progress?

Well, yes and no. We should applaud ourselves if we've shown up to our life purpose actions, whether or not we've made that much tangible progress. If you're dieting and hit a plateau—which means that although you eat carefully all week, you don't lose a single pound—that should count as a good week.

On the other hand, we do want to make progress. So, let us think about the idea of milestones. Milestones are markers on your life journey. Each one of your life purposes will have different milestones, and a given life purpose may have multiple milestones, depending on how you craft and define that purpose. Each life purpose choice and each life purpose sub-choice requires its own careful milestone consideration.

For instance, your physical health life purpose choice may be made of a diet component, an exercise component, a sleep component, and so on. Each of those can and will have their own milestones. Your creativity life purpose choice may be made of a regular painting practice, a regular writing practice, and regular piano practice. Each of those can and will have their own milestones. Your career life purpose choice may be made up of job satisfaction, conflict resolution, and pay advancement. Each of these can and will have their own milestones.

Are milestones always a "numbers" sort of thing: how many pounds lost, how many days you worked on writing your novel, how often you and your spouse went out on a date, how many days this month you meditated, and so on? Or can they also be articulated as levels, stages, and in many other ways; for instance, as in the levels leading up to a black belt in karate or as a new job position or job title at work? Well, both ways make sense!

Your deep dive task is to make sense of what milestones you want to attach to each of your life purposes. Some will be numeric milestones, and some will sound different from numbers. For instance, you might set a milestone with respect to the novel that you're writing for getting a first draft of it done. Or you might set weekly milestones to write four days every week. Or you might set a milestone of entering a writing competition during the next three months. Or you might set a milestone to complete the first 10,000 words of your draft. Or you might choose all of these! See how that works?

A particular milestone might be a number, or it might be created in some other way. For instance, you might create your own job satisfaction rating scale and track your satisfaction numerically, aiming at "8" or "9" as milestones (and "10" as an ultimate goal). Or you might designate specific levels of satisfaction as your milestones, aiming for "high" as your ultimate goal and "more satisfied for two consecutive weeks" as your next milestone. These are the kinds of choices that you get to make as you create your milestones.

Try this now: for each of your life purpose choices (and for each of your sub-life purpose choices, like dieting or exercise under health), consider what milestones you'd like to create. Hold this as a creative act and a creative process, and enjoy your time identifying and creating these milestones. You do not need to do anything like a "perfect" job—you will understand this process much better as you actually live your live purposes. And naturally your milestones may (and likely will) change!

Consider the milestones that you create today as tentative milestones that need to be tested in the crucible of living. Maybe you've set the bar too high with a given milestone, or maybe you've set the bar too low. Maybe you've missed the mark entirely. All of that is fine and to be expected! Celebrate your efforts—and learn by living!

CHAPTER 62

SECOND INTERLUDE

We make our life purpose choices, somehow. We try to factor in value. We try to keep our ego in check. We try to make sense of the welter of possibilities that our brainstorming produces. We grapple with the fact that some purposes feel smallish, like increasing our exercise regimen from four days a week to five, and some seem monumental, like becoming the architect we've dreamed of being.

We do our tasks of translation, turning each life purpose choice into something that we can express, something with action steps attached, something that we can put on our schedule. We do our best to align our thoughts with those choices. We do some calming work. What a lot we've done!

Then, we try to live those purposes. And you may find yourself quite reluctant to make that effort. Why? Because by naming your life purposes, you've set the bar very high. If, let's say, you assert that your primary life purpose is to do the next right thing, then you have to do the next right thing. It was fine, even inspiring, to put it on paper. Now you have to get up and do things!

And you must keep at it, one next right thing after another next right thing, forever. How much work you have made for yourself! Wouldn't it be ever so much easier just to keep seeking meaning and purpose, even if there is nothing to find? But you really know better than to keep seeking. You know to choose and act. If only you could get off the sofa!

If you say that one of your life purposes is to write fiction in your most passionate and powerful voice, well, then you have to sit there, day in and day out, on the many bad days as well as on the good ones, and struggle to write that powerful fiction. That's what you've gotten yourself into!

If you announce that you want to love and be loved, you have to actually love and you actually have to be loveable. This may necessitate a huge personality upgrade and some real movement away from grandiosity, arrogance, narcissism, and other ego-driven traits. You may have to change how you speak, how you think, and how you act. Gosh! Did putting "to love and be loved" on a piece of paper sign you up for all that!

These are not easy things. Making life purpose choices sets us up for real work. You decide to be a better parent—and then you have your actual kids to deal with. You decide to be an activist—and then you have to put your body on the line. No wonder that you may find yourself reluctant to move from that lovely list to the reality of action.

Let us be simple. Let us plan for one week—just one week. Let's get some number of your life purposes penciled in; maybe not all of them—maybe just three. Let's pick three. How about the ones that top your list, health, creativity, and service? Let's get those three, expressed as clear, real-world actions, onto your weekly calendar.

Let's get exercise penciled in. Let's get musical practice penciled in. Let's get two volunteer hours penciled in. Okay? Let's add just a few more bells and whistles: a daily life purposes check-in first thing each day, so as to orient yourself in the direction of your life purposes; and maybe a reflection at the end of the week, where you chat with yourself about the process? That would make for an excellent week!

And add a celebration! Make sure to pencil in a celebration—or many of them. If you find yourself living your life purposes, or coming close to living them, or even just making a valiant effort, celebrate that! A spoonful of whipped cream? A dance around the living room? High-fiving yourself? Any movement you manage to make, from naming your life purposes to actually living them out, deserves at least some cherries and blueberries!

CHAPTER 63

SUPPORT I: YOUR LIFE PURPOSES STATEMENT

A life purposes statement is nothing like a life purpose statement. The notion of a life purpose statement implies that you can reduce your life to one singular purpose. You can't. A life purposes statement, by contrast, accompanies you as you live the project of your life and provides a handy reminder of some headlines that you'd like to remember. It is a reminder, not a final answer.

The one I like to suggest is, "Do the next right thing." "Do the next right thing" reminds you that you'd prefer to live an ethical life rather than an unprincipled one. But it does more than that. It suggests what an interesting word "right" can be. "Right" can mean "ethical." But "right" can also mean "strategic," or "appropriate," or even "out-of-the-box." It is one rich word!

Let's say that you've worked hard at one of your life purposes. The next right thing might be a snack, a hot shower, or a nap. These aren't moral choices, but they are contextually the next right things for you to do to keep yourself on track, prepare you to tackle the next life purpose on your list, and help you maintain a kind of balance between engagement and disengagement—between intensity and relaxation.

The next right thing might even be something impulsive, because you need to break free just a little bit from your wise, regimented life. It might be something a little indulgent after a week of supreme carefulness. "Right" has a beautiful richness to it, because what it is means as part of your life purposes statement is that you are keeping track of your life moment by moment: you know what you need, you know what to do, you know how to live.

Naming your life purposes involves connecting the dots between your desires and appetites; your dreams and goals; your values, principles, and intentions; and everything else pressing down on you and welling up within you. If you were to try to *really* connect all those dots—if, for example, you were to create a document as long as a technical manual by which to live—you would likely never dip into that manual, nor find a way to make good use of it. The better answer—and a really good answer—is to keep it simple.

The approach we will take to reach this "simplicity" is something I am calling a life purposes statement. In one great gulp, you take into account the values you want to uphold, the dreams and goals you have for yourself, the vision you have for how you carry yourself in the world, and spend whatever time it takes to turn that unwieldy, contradictory material into a coherent statement that expresses your core decisions about your life.

"Do the next right thing" is one possibility. But the choice is yours; there are no rules or regulations. A few suggestions, though: you probably want to keep it short; it would be lovely if it is a bit memorable; and you might give your newly written statement a trial period of a day or so to see if it is doing the work you want it to do, reminding you of your life purposes and supporting your efforts. If it seems not to be quite working, try again!

Here are seven that clients of mine have created. Pamela: "Action and satisfaction, today and every day." Sylvia: "I bring my complete self to each moment." Lois: "Right here, right now, paying attention and making meaning." Harrison: "Years of creating a body of work, days of grace and enthusiasm." Judy: "Passion and presence, courage and conviction." Frank: "I take pride in working with my hands and doing the right thing." Sonia: "I am at ease in the universe, as long as I speak in my own voice."

Think of those rich slogans from AA: "First things first," "One day at a time," and "Easy does it." They don't say everything that might be said about the recovery process, nor everything that might be said about how you want to live your life. But they are wonderfully effective reminders. They are useful, powerful, and beautiful.

Try your hand at creating yours. Living your life purposes requires support—from you. One tool in your support tool kit is your life purposes statement; take the time to find those few words that do a grand job of reminding you that your life is your project and is in your own hands, and that you mean to live your life purposes. Provide yourself with that sort of compact, portable help.

CHAPTER 64

SUPPORT II: YOUR LIFE PURPOSES ICON

Here is another excellent way to support your intention to live your life purposes every day. Think of the way that a Christian cross or a Jewish Star of David holds a wealth of meaning for Christians and Jews. For the religious, these iconic symbols carry volumes of information in a simple, portable, brilliant way about what life means and about how to live. Don't those icons do a ton of work?

Other life purpose icons include the clenched fist of Black power, the dove of peace, the image of the Buddha, and the rainbow flag of gay rights. These images provide a wealth of information and meaning for those people for whom they are personally symbolic. Does the image of the Buddha mean the exact same thing to any two Buddhists? No. But does it hold meaning for each? Yes!

Such life purpose icons abound. But rarely does an individual create and make use of a personal icon that she employs to encapsulate her life purposes. People tend never to do this because it doesn't occur to them to do so. It is not an assignment any fifth-grade teacher ever gave them. It is not something that was ever discussed over Sunday dinner. It just never came up.

Even if it did occur to them to create their own personal life purposes icon, they might still feel challenged to accept that they have the right to create something as weighty as a Christian cross or a Jewish Star of David. Some thought like "How dare I?" might leap to mind; especially if they've gotten in the unfortunate habit of suppressing their individuality, that long-standing habit might stop them in their tracks.

However, you not only have that right, you have the obligation to hold your personal life purposes as exactly that important! And so, what might you choose? Well, literally anything under the sun. The world of images is your oyster. Close your eyes, mind your breath for a moment, and let an image rise to the occasion. How exciting for you!

Here are a few examples from others who have envisioned an icon for their life purposes:

Paula, a painter: "My life purpose icon is the walking stick. I have a walking stick in real life, and I treasure it. It is somewhat crooked, as is the path of life. But it is sturdy, and I cannot break it. It is made of both light and dark wood, representing life's dualities—day and night, stormy and peaceful, happy and full of strife. And it was born from something rooted to this earth, just as I am."

Sandra, a sculptor: "My personal icon is a lighthouse. A lighthouse is steadfast. A lighthouse stands out and stands alone. And a lighthouse has its own beauty and strength. It's built to withstand the worst storms, it's a fantastic design with a tremendously useful function, and it's a genuinely positive image."

Kimberly, an aeronautical engineer: "I've chosen a rocket as my life purposes icon. My favorite fantasy is to see the earth from space. Just as ships are built to sail the seas rather than languish in harbors, rockets are built to blast off rather than stand on the launch pad. Yes, mistakes will be made, postponements will happen, and problems will arise—but persistence pays off when we blaze into the unknown."

Imagine that you could carry your life purposes around with you in a portable way by creating your own icon. What might you choose? A walking stick, a polished stone, a lighthouse, a rocket, a hummingbird, a throne, an egg—what might your life purposes icon be? Stop for a moment. Maybe one will come to you just like that, like a bolt of lightning. Maybe it will *be* a bolt of lightning!

And how might you carry it around and keep it close? By making it into a necklace that you wear daily, or a ring? Perhaps by making it your screensaver image? Could you sculpt or paint it and keep the sculpture on your desk or the painting across from your bed? What if you could see it every morning when you awoke? Wouldn't that orient you in a brilliant direction?

CHAPTER 65

SUPPORT III: YOUR LIFE PURPOSES MANTRA

A mantra might also support you. A mantra is either something you repeat, or words (or a sound) to which you repeatedly listen because you find that it serves you to hear them. It could be a sound, a word, a phrase, or a whole passage. It isn't its size or the shape that determines whether something is or isn't a mantra. It's whether it serves you to hear it.

Perhaps a reminder of your many life purposes can be captured by a sound: could it be the sound of wind chimes, some notes of music, a single harmonious tone, or a bird's song? Is there something short, sweet, and memorable that evokes the feeling of your life purposes? Are you hearing something like that in your mind's ear right now?

The world is full of mournful sounds, evocative sounds, memorable sounds: train whistles, a screen door closing, a baby laughing. Record a sound that moves you and listen to it. Do you even have to record it? Can't you just hear it? And if you can whistle...

Or your mantra could be a word. It could be a word like *om*, courage, now, hope, or amazing. If shamanism holds power for you, it could be the name of your power animal—jaguar, crow, cougar, lynx, eagle. Maybe it's a place: Paris, a fjord, a valley. Or a principle: fairness, liberty, justice. Is a word coming to mind?

For me, the word is "process." "Process" is my mantra. If something hasn't worked—if a paragraph is off, if a class hasn't filled, if a day got lost—I will intone, "Process." I know what I mean by that. It reminds me that progress is not linear, that showing up is the name of the game, and that magic can happen out of the blue at any given moment.

Your most powerful mantra might be your own name. Think of that! What might do a better job of carrying your life purposes, your identity, and your intentions than your own name? Wouldn't it be wonderful to have your name do that work? Say your name a few times in this new, mantra-like way. Does that work for you?

Or it could be a name you call yourself. Maybe your given name doesn't work for you. Maybe you don't much like the people who gave it to you or what seems like a mean-spirited choice on their part. How dare they name you after a fruit, a month, a gemstone, or a Brooklyn neighborhood? Flatbush—really? Why not call yourself something else and make your new name your mantra!

Or it could be a phrase. The life organization phrase that I've suggested you employ is "Do the next right thing." As a mantra, this could be shortened to "Next right thing" or "Right thing." Doesn't "right thing" have a ring to it? Might that serve you?

For me, a passage that reminds me of my life purpose choices is a line from a Paul Verlaine poem. The line is "*Il pleure dans mon coeur comme il pleut sur la ville,*" which roughly translates as "It cries in my heart as it rains on the town," and which is beautiful in French.

I can't tell you why this mournful line works so beautifully for me. But it does. When I hear myself saying it, I am refreshed, reminded, and reoriented. "Process" works for me, as does that line of poetry. So do bits of Motown lyrics and certain fragments of lines from novels. Let your mind wander. What are you hearing?

CHAPTER 66

SUPPORT IV: YOUR LIFE PURPOSES JOURNAL

You may already journal. Or you may never have had a desire to journal. Let me present the idea of a life purposes journal, one you keep that is devoted to your reflections about how choosing and living your life purposes is going. Like your life purposes icon, your life purposes statement, and your life purposes mantra, your life purposes journal might do a lovely job of helping support you in your effort to live purposefully.

You might check in with yourself each evening after what may have been an otherwise tumultuous or over-busy day, spending a few quiet, thoughtful minutes processing the day and reflecting on how living your intentions went. Did you, for instance, get to your business-building activities? If so, celebrate for a second. Maybe dance around the room. Celebrating these small daily victories could amount to one of your more important practices.

Did you get to your business-building activities but sourly and "against your will"? Then remind yourself that living your life purposes doesn't come with a guarantee that you will always be in a good mood. Nod; remind yourself of that truth; and congratulate yourself on successfully showing up. Living a given life purpose may make you grumpy, or possibly anxious, and it may activate some addictive craving. All of that can happen.

Maybe you've been thinking about peanuts all day long. But you survived; and now you get to reflect during your evening journal writing about how intentional living can make for days of this sort. You get to say a kind word to yourself; you can congratulate yourself for another day spent exactly as you intend to spend your days. Yes, you may be quite tired and a little out of sorts. But the day was a victory.

That's daily life purposes journaling. Maybe you'll also adopt a separate weekly life purposes journaling practice. You could use weekly journaling for more in-depth reflection than your daily life purposes journaling, taking time to reflect on the past week and plan for the new week. Here you get to consider why you were able to exercise on Tuesday and Thursday but not on Wednesday and maybe discover that Wednesdays present certain built-in obstacles that you hadn't noticed before. That's valuable insight!

This weekly reflection affords you the opportunity to do what is in fact quite a complicated thing to accomplish; namely, keeping track of your multiple life purposes. Maybe you automatically and intuitively track one or two of your life purposes, but what about life purposes three, four, and five? They may well need more mindful attention than life purposes one and two, and your weekly life purposes reflection is your opportunity to keep track of them.

Set the intention for this to be a gentle reflection, one full of self-forgiveness and ease, because it is completely likely that you will not have lived your week exactly as you had hoped or intended to live it. Indeed, it may have fallen far short of any ideal. Maybe you missed attending to almost all your life purposes in the hurly-burly of living. That happens! Do not beat yourself up if this occurred.

If that's how your week's been, you want to notice it but not dwell on how it fell short. Smile a little at how human plans get bashed about in the living, think carefully about how to make your coming week better, and recommit to this, the project of your life. Forgive yourself and recommit. Those are two steps of this dance!

You might want to also add another journaling practice, a monthly journaling check-in. It might serve you beautifully to provide yourself with a snapshot of how the month went. It might become clear that a particular life purpose needs more attention, or that a life purpose isn't feeling very important at the moment. Perhaps a life purpose monopolized your time, maybe in a good way, as a productive obsession, or maybe as a thief, stealing your time. Those would be good things to know!

Journaling brings with it real benefits. It allows you to get things off your chest, as well as helps you to form new intentions and recommit to your life purposes. The process also helps you to gain insight and better understand what's working and what isn't working in your life. Even an intermittent life purposes journaling practice might serve you beautifully. Just keep your life purposes journal handy and have the occasional fruitful conversation with yourself.

CHAPTER 67

EIGHT PRACTICES

There is no one, prescribed way to live—nor can there be. There are no particular things that you are obliged to do at four o'clock in the morning, at two in the afternoon, or at ten at night. You do not need to turn east, west, north, or south. You do not need to come together or stay apart. That is between you and you.

But while there are no prescribed things to do, there are many wise things to do. I think that all of the following are wise. See if you think so, too. None of these are obligatory. But all make sense, I think. Try some out, if you like. If one serves you, keep it; if it doesn't, discard it.

Practice One: Increase your life purposes vocabulary. Insert phrases like "absurd rebellion," "self-obligation," "meaning opportunities," "meaning investments," and "life purposes" into your internal conversations. Focus on a word like "individuality" or a phrase, such as "multiple life purpose choices." Learn this language.

Practice Two: Check in each morning—start every day with a life purposes check-in. Have a seat and remind yourself of your current life purpose choices. You might mindfully select the ones you intend to champion on that day, or simply stretch and wonder: "What are my life purpose efforts for today?" Wouldn't that contemplation serve you better than turning on the news?

Practice Three: Practice doing the next right thing. First, have a conversation with yourself about what the phrase "do the next right thing" signifies to you. Doing the next right thing is an art form, not a slogan! It is a big, wonderful, humane intention, albeit one that conflicts with our selfish genes and our rapacious appetites. Therefore, it needs a lot of practice.

Practice Four: Create a daily morning practice to do first thing each day in the service of your life purposes. This daily practice might be focused on creativity, health, career-building, mindfulness, working towards a personality upgrade, or whatever fits your life purposes. You would wake up and go directly to your practice. Maybe you will decide on a few different morning practices, providing you with multiple daily meaning opportunities. This could be a really positive addition to your day.

Practice Five: Take time to redesign your mind. You can get a better grip on your mind than is usually supposed by shooting for the high-bar goal of banishing thoughts that don't serve you and only thinking thoughts that actually do serve you. At the same time, you might use creative visualization to redesign your mind's interior by adding in windows that let in a welcome breeze, installing a virtual easy chair, painting those dingy walls a bright white, and so on. For more on this technique, see my book *Redesign Your Mind*.

Practice Six: Consider how energy management could help you live your life purposes. What might that look like? Begin by making a two-column list, dividing activities and habits into those that drain your energy and those that increase your energy. That would be a start! Energy is a particularly mysterious part of the human story, an aspect that is a challenge both to grasp and to manage. Is it time to learn more about it?

Practice Seven: Practice surrendering to not knowing. This would help you to more calmly tolerate all that is not known and never can be known. You might begin to softly murmur, "I just don't know about that," rather than becoming disoriented. Maybe you'll create a daily ceremony of surrender to not knowing, perhaps including bowing in the direction of mystery or nodding at the inexplicable.

Practice Eight: You might practice choosing "love" as a life purpose and a meaning opportunity. All that would be required is a softening of your heart and an object of affection. If you bestow love today, you may coax some new meaning into existence. And you could do that again tomorrow. Think of words in the family of love: affection, kindness, generosity, intimacy. They paint a picture of what loving looks like.

CHAPTER 68

MOMENTS OF JOY

I have been making so much work for you! But some of the payoffs from all this work may be joy, pleasure, and happiness. Any one of your life purpose choices is a possible source of joy. To live your life purposes is to promote joy. And while moments of joy may be few and far between, they are among our human riches.

Our child marries. The ceremony is very brief, lasting hardly five minutes. But those few minutes can be as rich as any moments can be, and, somewhere within us, they last forever. How can you calculate the value of something that lasts a second but that also lasts forever? Isn't it worth doing all the work of living your life purposes to experience that happiness?

Moments of joy, suddenly here and suddenly gone, are not just passing moments—they are momentous. And so, we covet them, we prize them, and we angle for them. If we rarely or never experience them, we step to the side and try to figure out why. No joy? No pleasure? No happiness? Why?

We have available to us that step to the side, the step we take to provide ourselves with the time and the space to practice awareness. How many more joys and pleasures might we experience if we stepped to the side and took careful stock? We might discover, for instance, that we are talking ourselves out of joy. How terrible!

Say that you've been living one of your life purposes by writing your novel. You write for an hour and then stop to make yourself a cup of tea. As the water boils, you might worry that what you just wrote was terrible.

That might be your usual thinking. Or you could feel some joy at having honorably worked. Wouldn't that be better?

Imagine! There you are standing in the kitchen, waiting for the water to boil, and instead of beating yourself up about your last few paragraphs or shaking your fist at the publishing gods, you allow yourself a moment of joy at having written. Wonderful!

You just got a precious moment of joy by allowing for it. If you rarely allow for joy, what exactly is going to feel joyous? Will that delicious soup bring you joy if your mind is completely elsewhere? Will your child's sudden smile, if you are always in the other room?

Maybe the very idea that you can intentionally stand ready to notice joy and to experience joy is worth promoting to the high place of a life purpose choice. More pleasure, please. More joy, please. More happiness, please. You could do the opposite; you could opt to feel miserable. But is that the next right thing? Is that the life purpose choice you want to be making?

Joy, pleasure, satisfaction, happiness, elation, ecstasy—what important words! Let us do the principled thing, and we are then also gifted with happiness; mustn't that be the very pinnacle of human existence? We do not chase happiness as if it were a bright shiny object. We simply live according to our chosen purposes, bringing our mindful attention to the present moment. And if joy arrives, what a blessing!

Consider making openness to joy a life purpose choice. You can't make joy happen, any more than you can make meaning happen. But you can create opportunities for joy, just as you can create opportunities for meaning. Make a list right now: what are some opportunities for joy?

CHAPTER 69

NEGOTIATING AND NAVIGATING EACH DAY

When you live the way that I'm describing, each day is a kind of negotiation. You negotiate with yourself which of your life purposes you intend to live on that day, what the exact actions are that go with those choices, how long you'll spend on this or that purpose, and which portions of the day must be surrendered to the other tasks of living.

Maybe you've found the way to have every single thing you do fall under the heading of a life purpose. Maybe getting stuck in commuter traffic connects to "chance to think about the novel I'm writing and make some audio notes," and sweeping the hall connects to "calmly and mindfully handling the ordinary tasks of living." Maybe you've found a way to live the phrase "do the next right thing" so that everything you do feels purposeful. That would be lovely!

But if you haven't arrived at that seamless place, then you have the job of juggling, calculating, and managing projects. You pencil in a forty-minute walk around the neighborhood as the exact action that corresponds to your "health and fitness" life purpose. You schedule an hour of reading with your daughter at seven in the evening as the exact action that matches your "parenting" life purpose. As you contemplate a career change, you pencil in that hour of blue-sky thinking as the action that is right to support your "career" life purpose, and so on.

You negotiate each day, making daily choices and painting yourself a daily picture of how that day will look. Then you navigate that day as life throws you curve balls; and your own personality may resist tackling a task or balk at "all this regimentation" as some spontaneous desire or inspiration sends you off in an unexpected direction. You have your template for the day, which you negotiated with yourself first thing that morning, and then you must navigate your actual day, which will likely be its own kind of subtle rollercoaster.

As you deal with this negotiating and navigating, you stay mindful of which life purposes aren't making it onto your to-do list for that day. Is this another day on which you didn't manage to get to "service" or "activism," not to mention "relaxation" or "relationships"? You may want to create a way of noting all that, maybe in a "life purposes weekly planner," so that at the end of each week you have a record of which of your life purposes you attended to and which were for whatever reason avoided or skipped.

Maybe upon noting which life purposes were avoided or skipped, you would stop right then and there and make a point of scheduling those missed life purposes into your calendar for the coming week. This is another useful negotiation, as you plan out the coming week while trying your best to make sense of the many things that are important to you and how they can fit into just so many hours. Can you pay a little attention to each? Or would it work better to give a lot of attention to one pressing purpose and stay relaxed about the missed ones? Or is it possible to get up a little earlier to make more time for purposes that need more attention? Bring your creativity and resourcefulness to this process.

Maybe you would find it useful to do this life purposes updating on a monthly basis as well as weekly. Perhaps once a month, say on a Sunday afternoon, you might take yourself to your favorite café, review how your month went, and make some calculations and some new decisions about the coming month. Will you be able to create a "perfect" month? No. But you can do that most honorable thing: take charge of your life purposes as well as life and time will allow.

You are negotiating not as a cruel taskmaster to yourself but as a loving helpmate. You are completely on your own side, wanting nothing but the best for yourself. Yes, that "best" involves work, as living your life purposes is work. But there is no wicked stepmother from some grim fairy tale negotiating your schedule. This is your loving self, your best nature, your wisest mind aiding you in living the life that you know that you want to live. These are heartfelt calculations.

You've made your calculations—and then your real day happens. You know what will happen next: life. Maybe you will get a call that your elderly mother has fallen. Maybe you will suddenly remember that you need to go online and pay the car insurance premium. Maybe a bit of news will pass by your eyes, informing you of another attack on your civil liberties. Or possibly nothing more dramatic will happen than finding you have run out of your favorite tea. Will that necessitate an emergency run to the market? Such is a day!

Such an intentionally negotiated and navigated day is a kind of masterpiece—a masterpiece in living. It will likely have been a flawed masterpiece, because of course there will have been tasks that were avoided, those quarter hours lost to who knows what, that thing that took three times longer than you thought it would take, and so on. Of course. Days are like that. A negotiated and navigated day is not a flawless day. But it is a beautiful thing.

CHAPTER 70

CHANGED CIRCUMSTANCES

Many things in life change, in turn affecting our life purpose choices. For example, consider society itself. Societies regularly change, often for the worse. Society is no benign thing. Nations, tribes, work cultures, fraternal organizations, religious sects, communes, country clubs, towns, and neighborhoods all stand poised to judge, silence, and ostracize their members. At any moment, they may become meaner and stricter than they previously were. This will naturally affect your life purpose choices!

Can you plot your escape from your own society and culture? It's unlikely that you can. How, for instance, will you get sufficient funding for your science lab if you don't play the game of grant proposals and kowtow to funders? How will you travel from here to there without the travel documents that societies demand, all those passports, visas, and identity cards? You can't really escape society and culture.

Your society may become more repressive and authoritarian. That happens. Societies are rather authoritarian by their nature and habit, and you, by contrast, are likely anti-authoritarian by nature and habit. So, you may find yourself in a tense, adversarial relationship with your own society. And when it veers in a more totalitarian direction, that shift can bring with it changed circumstances that may cause you to alter your vision of what's important. Maybe "resistance fighter" wasn't on your list of life purposes before—and now it is.

Major changes in life circumstances include divorce, job loss, a chilling medical diagnosis, the death of a loved one, a major financial loss, and your nest emptying of children, as well as "positives" like retirement, a career leap forward, or a lottery win. Even something the size of a dog barking constantly next door or a shift at work—either reducing or increasing your duties and responsibilities—may alter your inner landscape and change what you consider important. The list of the sorts of changed circumstances that might affect you is longer than your arm!

Certain profound changes in circumstances can be subtle and can happen over a protracted period of time. Maybe your teaching job served you beautifully twenty years ago, but now it is an unpleasant grind. No single event caused you to change your mind and your feelings about teaching. But your thoughts and feelings about teaching are definitely different now. Teaching is now important to you only as a paycheck. Mustn't you bravely take this change into account as you calculate your current life purpose choices?

Our very personality can change, amounting to another kind of changed circumstances. Yesterday, we drank alcoholically. Today, we are in the first day of recovery. A year from now, we will have achieved a year of sobriety. Ten years from now, we'll have ten years of sobriety under our belt. As the strength of our recovery grows, our circumstances change. We're now in a position to remain gainfully employed, to enter into an intimate relationship, to reconnect with our estranged children. Personality, changed circumstances, and life purposes connect.

Think of how a single changed circumstance might affect all of your life purpose choices. Career is important to you. Being an involved grandparent is important to you. Your health is important to you. Your friendships are important to you. Your home church is important to you. One day, you're offered the chance to manage your company's office in a country seven thousand miles away. You know that this move will advance your career, and conversely, if you refuse, you know your refusal will negatively impact your career. Plus, the proposed move is to a city notorious for its astounding pollution. What to do?

Your health is important to you. Move to a polluted city? Your home church, your friends, and your grandkids are important to you. Move seven thousand miles away from them? Your career is important to you.

But is it this important? Plus, you notice how other feelings have been activated: a dormant love of adventure, a long-forgotten ache to see more of the world, some sense that your life abroad will feel meaningful, and some desire to break out of the comfortable rut in which you've been living. What is more important than what? What is most important?

Can rationality even be applied here? How do you weigh grandkids against an adventure? A polluted city against meaningfulness? Your home church against a pay hike that assures your retirement? An existentialist would say, "You are completely free to choose." Ha! Yes, you are completely free to choose. But does this sort of predicament feel more like freedom or like crisis?

Or does it perhaps feel like anxiety? Deciding whether to take that job seven thousand miles away and leave everything behind or stay put and stall one's career is a choice that can bring with it all sorts of whole-body effects. It can make us sweat; it can make us dizzy. It can make us want to drink. It can make us fly off on a misadventure. It can flat-out put us in a panic.

I've left anxiety out of our discussion so far, but not because it doesn't thread its way through this process. It surely does. Anxiety is a feature of the human condition. Anxiety warns us that we're in danger, or that we think we're in danger. Anxiety is our body's full-throated announcement to take care, to flee, to fight, to do something. Do we suppose that anxiety will accompany our changed circumstances?

Changed circumstances will alter the complexion of your life purpose choices. Their order, their importance, and their connections to one another may shift. This or that choice may pull a vanishing act. This or that choice may unexpectedly appear. When your circumstances change significantly, your menu of life purpose choices may look one way before and very, very different after. And yes, you will not feel ready! Bet on it.

CHAPTER 71

AGE AND STAGE

You may remember the beautiful job that the psychologist Erik Erikson did of describing what he called "the eight stages of psychosocial adjustment," each with its different possible outcomes. These possible outcomes included trust versus mistrust, autonomy versus shame, initiative versus guilt, industry versus inferiority, intimacy versus isolation, and so on; a very interesting scheme!

His model reminds us how different our tasks and purposes can be from one age to another and from one stage of life to another. Parenting may have had no particular place on our list of life purpose choices. Then a child unexpectedly arrives, and everything shifts. Now career matters considerably more than it did before, because we have new responsibilities and another mouth to feed. Of course, parenting suddenly matters. Maybe friendships wane—who has the time? Sleep becomes more important than friendships! And so it goes.

Having adventures may be a prime life purpose at the age of eighteen. How well will that fit with your putative priority of getting a college education? Will you prefer going to class—or driving fast down the road with your new college buddies? Can college and adventures coexist? Can you keep the adventures "safe" and avoid the dangers of addiction, round-the-clock wakefulness, or an unwanted pregnancy? How will you navigate and negotiate that tumultuous age and stage?

Maybe you've chosen a profession where it's hard to make a living—say, you've chosen to act. It may feel fine for some number of years to live in poverty and work menial jobs while trying to make it as an actor. But if you don't find success, or enough success, how long can or should your desire to act remain a life purpose choice? Forever? Even if it is costing you a tremendous amount? Even if it means passing up other possibly really important life purpose opportunities?

No children—because of acting? No heat in the winter—because of acting? These are the sorts of conflicts and conundrums that confront us over the long haul of life purpose decisions. We make our choices, we live them—and we suffer them. We revisit them, we rethink them, we recommit to them, we abandon them. Three things happen: we learn more, our circumstances change, and we move to the next stage of life—all simultaneously!

Think about the long haul of your own life. Even if you are still young, you have lived. At the age of six, what would your list of life purpose choices have contained? What about at fifteen, or twenty-one, or twenty-six, or thirty-two? How about later in life? You might find it eye-opening to try to create those lists. Were you even the same person from age to age and stage to stage?

At the age of thirteen, I was a high school student at a math and science high school, on the road to astrophysics. At the age of nineteen, I was a platoon sergeant in Korea. At the age of twenty-three, I was a new father in a sudden marriage that would soon be ending. At twenty-eight, I was living alone in an apartment with rats, writing fiction. And so on. Think of your life. Is it a straight line or a strange line? I'm betting on strange.

In addition to creating your list of life purpose choices, getting them onto your daily calendar, and actually living them, you might ask yourself, "Who am I at this stage of my life?" Get ready to surprise yourself. You may have a mental image of yourself from five years ago or ten years ago, one that you haven't found a moment to update. I know that I was using a promotional headshot for ten years without finding the right moment to replace it! Take some time and catch up with yourself. Who are you today?

Stages creep and blend. We still feel young—until we look in the mirror. We still feel agile—until we try to go out for a pass at the annual Thanksgiving family football game. We still feel mentally sharp—until our car keys keep disappearing. We still feel attractive—except that no one is noticing us. This is life, part upward spiral, part decline, part tornado.

Over the long haul, we are wrenched by reality, blindsided by our changing needs and wants, confronted by new challenges, and forced to reevaluate our priorities and even our principles, and all the while completely unable to get off the rollercoaster of life. At every age and stage, choices confront us. Avoiding them isn't the answer. Rather, we try to face them head-on as best we can, making the appropriate, updated choices from exactly where we find ourselves.

CHAPTER 72

LIFE, SURFING

What does success look like when it comes to life purpose choosing? It looks like a life well lived—or an approximation of that, given our human nature and our inevitable shortfalls. We do not measure its success by the amount of happiness we've experienced or by the number of our accomplishments. We say, "Have I lived on purpose?" If we can answer yes—that is success.

An existentially successful life, one that makes us proud and provides us with the sorts of satisfactions that we've come to understand matter to us—the satisfactions of love, of service, of self-actualization, of shared caring, and others—is available to each of us. That isn't the same as an outwardly successful life punctuated by mansions and dream vacations. It is a life of quiet, personal meaning, where living our life purposes amounts to success.

It looks like a life where we can truthfully say, "I've tried to live this life of mine according to my principles and values, making tons of decisions in the dark, crossing my fingers, and standing up as best as I could to the vagaries of life and to my own pulls and cravings." Maybe we have only begun to live that way recently. Maybe years and decades went by lived less well than that. But if we can truthfully say that about now, that is something!

Success means coping with our own moods and thoughts, confronting our personality, dealing with our circumstances, and handling interactions with other human beings. We are obliged to do as much as the mythical Sisyphus, in our own way, carrying our own rocks, on some days completely unable to smile, on other days just a little amused at this human spectacle and our place in it.

I deem myself successful when I have a session with a coaching client and that person is helped, when I tell my grandkids an improvised tale and they are enthralled, or when I skip that unhealthy snack that I crave so very badly. I am proud when I contribute to a cause, even if it is just money and not blood, or when I rebel absurdly against an entrenched institution, even if I don't move the meter a millimeter. And you?

I've asked you to choose your life purposes and live them. Have good things happened already? Has anything changed for the better as you've wended your way through this book? To be sure, maybe nothing dramatic has occurred so far. Or maybe there have been some dramatic shifts and changes already? That would be exceptional!

Take a walk through your life purpose choices. For each one, what might success look like? Maybe each one comes with a variety of possible successful outcomes; what are they? Take a moment and announce what success will look like to you for each one of your life purposes. What will your mini milestones be, your small victories? Think about it!

Is there some crowning achievement we're after, some Nobel Prize for living? Is success managing those ten thousand steps to the top of the mountain? Should we be picturing some upward spiral from here to Heaven? No. We have our feet firmly planted on the ground, negotiating and navigating each day and paying attention to our life purposes, both to those that only take a moment, like hugging our child as she walks by, and to those that take a year or two, like writing our novel.

There is no mountain top. But there are ocean waves. The waves keep coming and crashing. Some waves are gentler, some gigantic. We ride all these waves. Maybe we have a quiet day of purposeful living. Lovely. And maybe we have a day of purposeful living that is also a day of crisis: a day with a challenging medical diagnosis or a career setback or a relationship cracking. Those are the waves. And our success is surfing those waves.

Of course, you get to define success for yourself. Maybe it doesn't look anything like my definition. That has been our story all along, the story of your radical self-authorship, the story of you being you. As we approach the end of this book, I want us to do a little bit of celebrating, celebrating that you and I have spent a little time together chatting about the important things. Wasn't that its own kind of success? I think so!

CHAPTER 73

LIFE, CHOSEN

Living your life in the way that I've been describing is a beautiful thing. To live without purpose is unlikely to work for you. Trying to find a singular "life's purpose" likely hasn't worked very well for you either, because there isn't one to find. This third way—you heroically living your multiple life purposes—is a better bet than living without purpose or chasing a single purpose.

To live knowing that you have many life purposes, that each one comes with nameable actions, and that every day you can attend to at least some of your life purposes, is to live about as well as a human being can live. To live a life where you consistently and adamantly choose your life purposes is to live a life of power and passion. You will feel alive, assured, and engaged. Excellent!

At the same time, I hope that you've arrived at the sophisticated understanding that your life purpose choices can't aspire to a kind of purity that human reality won't allow. Purposes can conflict and can contradict one another. Purposes can feel too hard, like too much heavy lifting in an already heavy life. This makes life purpose choosing a poignant affair.

It is no breeze or walk in the park. Yes, our choosing likely isn't as dramatic and terrible as the choice facing Sophie in William Styron's novel *Sophie's Choice*, where Sophie has to choose which of her children will live. Still, we must choose which of the things that are important to us will live. That is certainly dramatic to us. For us, our life is on the line.

This choosing is not in any way a dry affair or some rote cost/benefit analysis. It is as complicated as the universe itself. Stars colliding have nothing on the way our choices collide. We face choices like going to war for our country or taking care of our ailing mother. Should we stay at the same job until retirement or find a job we can better tolerate? Risk a difficult pregnancy, adopt a child, become foster parents, or none of the above? Such choices are hot to the touch, as hot, in their own way, as stars burning.

This makes their beauty akin to the night sky seen with the naked eye or the swirling of galaxies viewed through a telescope. They are as beautiful and as complicated as a single roiling human cell, as the flight of birds or the unfolding of plants, as anything that nature has created. Isn't the ability to make these choices for ourselves and test them in the living something like an honor bestowed on us by evolution?

I hope that you will not linger too long in thinking about all of this and will instead move on to the doing. There is magic in the doing. When you can spend the day attending to three or four of your life purposes, with the knowledge that you've accomplished such a high-bar, remarkable thing and can congratulate yourself even as fatigue washes over you, that is a good day. Have that day today, or, at the latest, tomorrow.

I thank you for taking this stroll with me through these existential fields. There have been daisies and poppies and bare branches and landmines. We have seen how meaning comes and goes, as is its nature, just as field creatures come and go, visible for a split second and then back underground again. We have faced reality without much blinking. I hope that you've enjoyed this stroll and that you've benefitted from it. Take care; just over the horizon, there will be more choices and more living.

RESOURCES AND FURTHER READING

Let me mention a few resources that may serve you.

First, you might like to help people who are trying to identify and live their life purposes. One way that you can be of help is by becoming an existential wellness coach. Existential wellness coaching is a new profession that combines ideas from life coaching, existential coaching, and wellness coaching. In conjunction with Noble-Manhattan Coaching, a worldwide training company, I've created an Existential Wellness Coach Certificate Program that may interest you. You can learn more about it at: wellnesscoachtraining.online.

(If you're not sure if coaching is something that you might like to do, or if you'd like to learn more about coaching, I recommend *The Coach's Way*, my guide to the coaching profession. In it, I describe in detail what coaches do, how they help, and how coaching sessions flow.)

Second, you might enjoy identifying your life purpose choices and tracking their progress by using the app Purposely, which I developed. Purposely helps you identify your life purposes, connect those purposes to specific daily, weekly, and monthly actions, and create milestones so that you can monitor your progress toward your various life purpose goals. It might serve your needs beautifully, so give it a peek. If you're a helping professional like a coach or a therapist, it may also meet your clients' needs as well.

Third, during the course of this book, I've mentioned many ideas and practices in passing. Let me guide you to some more reading where you can learn about these various ideas and practices:

- I mentioned how sleep thinking can be used to solve problems and identify life purposes. I present a whole program for encouraging and capturing your sleep thinking in *The Magic of Sleep Thinking*.

- I briefly discussed the idea of redesigning your mind, a visualization technique where you redesign and redecorate the "room that is your mind" so as to reduce anxiety and sadness and fundamentally change your thoughts. You can learn more about this technique in *Redesign Your Mind*.

- I discussed how you might want to make navigating and negotiating each day around your life purposes a regular daily practice. You might enjoy learning more about the elements of a daily practice in *The Power of Daily Practice*.

- Some of the challenges that arise which make it difficult for us to live our life purposes have to do with the fact that intelligence, sensitivity, and a creative nature bring with them additional challenges. I've described many of these additional challenges and what you can do about them in a pair of books, *Why Smart, Creative and Highly Sensitive People Hurt* and *Why Smart Teens Hurt*. I recommend them to you.

- Other challenges that arise have to do with our toxic relationships, family difficulties, and the authoritarians in our own family, authoritarians who may be bullying us and preventing us from living our purposes. I address these issues in a number of books, among them *Overcoming Your Difficult Family* and *Parents Who Bully*.

- Many people nowadays have received a mental disorder diagnosis, and that diagnosis has become part of their self-identity. They may now see themselves as "having" ADHD, PTSD, bipolar disorder, autism, obsessive-compulsive disorder, or one of the many other disorders described in the diagnostic guides that clinicians use. You may want to get clearer on what such diagnoses mean, since a better understanding of them can help motivate you to decide to choose and live your life purposes. Some of my books in this area include *Rethinking Depression*, *The Future of Mental*

Health, Humane Helping, and, as editor, *Deconstructing ADHD, Critiquing the Psychiatric Model*, and *Humane Alternatives to the Psychiatric Model*.

- As I've mentioned, anxiety is bound to thread through the process of choosing and living your life purposes. It naturally and likely inevitably will be present as you take on life purpose decisions. To learn more about how to deal with anxiety in simple, commonsense ways, please take a look at *Mastering Creative Anxiety*. While it is designed to address the specific anxiety issues of creatives, its robust toolbox of anxiety management strategies will serve you, too.

AN INVITATION TO GET IN TOUCH WITH ME

Please make sure to be in touch if you have any questions, thoughts, or experiences to share. I'd love to hear how the process of choosing and living your life purposes has gone for you. Let me know! And good luck on the project of your life!

—Eric Maisel

Email me at: ericmaisel@hotmail.com

www.ericmaisel.com

www.ericmaiselsolutions.com

On LinkedIn: https://linkedin.com/in/eric-maisel

On Facebook: www.facebook.com/eric.maisel

On Instagram and X [formerly Twitter]: @ericmaisel

ABOUT THE AUTHOR

Eric Maisel has written more than fifty books and has edited an additional dozen. He is the lead editor for the Ethics International Press Critical Psychology and Critical Psychiatry series, and his *Psychology Today* blog "Rethinking Mental Health" has drawn more than three million views. In conjunction with Noble-Manhattan Coaching, he has developed a pair of worldwide training programs: a Creativity Coach Certificate Program, and an Existential Wellness Coach Certificate Program.

Dr. Maisel regularly blogs for the Good Men Project and Fine Art America, as well as presenting sponsored workshops, webinars, and keynotes, he and maintains an international coaching practice. He has been interviewed more than five hundred times on the topics of creativity, life purpose, meaning, and mental health, and is currently developing a life organization app to be released in 2025.

mango
PUBLISHING

Mango Publishing, established in 2014, publishes an eclectic list of books by diverse authors—both new and established voices—on topics ranging from business, personal growth, women's empowerment, LGBTQ+ studies, health, and spirituality to history, popular culture, time management, decluttering, lifestyle, mental wellness, aging, and sustainable living. We were named 2019 *and* 2020's #1 fastest growing independent publisher by *Publishers Weekly*. Our success is driven by our main goal, which is to publish high-quality books that will entertain readers as well as make a positive difference in their lives.

Our readers are our most important resource; we value your input, suggestions, and ideas. We'd love to hear from you—after all, we are publishing books for you!

Please stay in touch with us and follow us at:

Facebook: Mango Publishing

Twitter: @MangoPublishing

Instagram: @MangoPublishing

LinkedIn: Mango Publishing

Pinterest: Mango Publishing

Newsletter: mangopublishinggroup.com/newsletter

Join us on Mango's journey to reinvent publishing, one book at a time.